ADVANCE PRAISE

"So many families will recognize themselves on these pages, as Jim narrates the big and small moments—some sorrowful, some surprisingly sweet—that punctuated pandemic life with young kids. A timely and universal read."

—Heidi Stevens, Journalist and Nationally Syndicated
Parenting Columnist

"Jim Schneider writes in a voice that is so friendly and charming, you can't help but grab his hand and let him lead you back through the worst of times: 2020-2021. On the outside, the world is on fire: COVID, George Floyd, vicious political division. On the inside, the Schneiders fight fires of their own: remote learning, stir-crazy kids, their son's autism diagnosis. *Fencebat: A Big Kid's Guide to Parenting, Personal Growth and Play* offers an earnest yet jovial male perspective on the insurmountable challenges of raising a family in a world wrought with strife."

—Heather Sabel Preston, Author, *Memoirs of a Hag*

"Jim captures the joy and chaos of parenting through the ins and outs of daily family life, as well as through one of the hardest times in history. Nestled inside the pandemic story is a personal one as Jim processes new knowledge about his son, Henry. Henry is autistic and like all parents receiving this news, Jim has questions. His ultimate answers are about hope and wonder and the remarkable person Henry is, ASD included. We appreciate Jim's honesty as he describes the ways his family embraces possibility and recommend it to anyone anywhere in the process of loving a child, without or without a disability, wholeheartedly."

—Tena M. Green and Hettie Hueber, M.Ed,
Educational Advocates, Moms and Founders of Inclusion
Dynamics Educational Advocacy (IDEA)

"Reading this book feels like talking to a friend. Jim Schneider imparts nuggets of wisdom while regaling us with stories about his family of four as they navigated the COVID-19 lockdown and slowly re-entered the world. Anyone, whether you're a parent or not, can identify with his stories, which Schneider was brilliant to record (with his wonderful sense of humor!) and consider during a time most of us would like to forget. He not only uncovers life's lessons in the mundane and even the traumatic, but Schneider also underscores joy is found in the little things that tend to go unnoticed each day. As we all dive into our new normal, Schneider's book will remind you to slow down, take a breath and enjoy all the fine details that make a life truly joyful."

—Christina Koch, Mom and Editorial Director
of Retrofit Magazine

"*Fencebat* offers an amusing reminder for all parents that sometimes you just need to allow yourself a little grace. While the stories within *Fencebat* are set during the pandemic, the life-lessons shared for parents are timeless. Jim's humorous and thoughtful look back at his family's journey through a COVID-infected world highlights the value in rediscovering the kid at heart that lives within us all. As Jim states so eloquently, ". . . no matter how dark our surroundings might be, it's in our power to create moments of laughter and joy." *Fencebat* has plenty of both."

—Tom Rosenthal, Dad and Assistant Director
Philanthropy Programs at Northwestern Mutual

"Jim's vivid and wry book invites us to relive his parenting discoveries, successes, and shortcomings without sugarcoating reality. It also stirs in us a yearning to recall our own endless hours of caregiving during and beyond the pandemic. As Jim details his family's jokes, bursts of sadness and joy, and moments that can't be made up—all of which typically disappear into the haze of life—you become inspired to crack open that dusty journal on your shelf."

—Wanda Lau, Mom and Editorial Director,
Endeavor Business Media

FENCEBAT

FENCEBAT

A BIG KID'S GUIDE TO PARENTING, PERSONAL GROWTH, AND PLAY

JIM SCHNEIDER

7430
— PRESS —

Fencebat: A Big Kid's Guide to Parenting, Personal Growth, and Play
Published by 7430 Press
Westminster, Colorado, U.S.A.

SCHNEIDER, JIM, Author
FENCEBAT
JIM SCHNEIDER

Library of Congress Control Number: 2022917350
ISBN: 979-8-9869753-1-3 (hardcover)
ISBN: 979-8-9869753-0-6, 979-8-9869753-3-7 (paperback)
ISBN: 979-8-9869753-2-0 (digital)

FAMILY & RELATIONSHIPS / Parenting / Fatherhood
BODY, MIND & SPIRIT / Inspiration & Personal Growth
BIOGRAPHY & AUTOBIOGRAPHY / Editors, Journalists, Publishers

Editing: PiquePublishing.com
Editing: GetFineLines.weebly.com
Design: ClarityDesignworks.com
Book Consulting: FinishTheBookPublishing.com
Photography: goodmorrowphotography.com

QUANTITY PURCHASES: Schools, companies, professional groups, clubs, and other organizations may qualify for special terms when ordering quantities of this title. For information, email info@7430Press.com.

To Erin, Amelia and Henry.
You are my greatest teachers, my inspiration,
and the only people on Earth
I'd want to be quarantined with for a year or two.
Thank you for supporting me,
for making me laugh, and helping me learn.

Fence: /fens/ *a barrier, railing, or other upright structure, typically of wood or wire, enclosing an area of ground to mark a boundary, control access, or prevent escape [Source: Oxford Languages]*

Bat: /bat/ *an implement with a handle and a solid surface, usually of wood, used for hitting the ball in games such as baseball, cricket, and table tennis. [Source: Oxford Languages]*

Fencebat: /fens–bat/ *a game invented during the COVID-19 pandemic of 2020 by two young children creatively fending off boredom, of which the object appears to be sticking a foam bat through the lats of a backyard fence as comically as possible. Extra points are earned for any configuration that makes it more difficult for Dad to remove the bat from the fence. [Source: Jim Schneider, author and father of Amelia and Henry, the founders of Fencebat.]*

CONTENTS

A NOTE FROM THE AUTHOR

This book is for all the parents out there who often feel lost, over-whelmed, and like they are making it up as they go. Parenting is high-wire improv before a live studio audience in the face of chaos. Let's be honest, none of us REALLY know what we're doing, we're just doing our best to learn from every stumble and do better the next day.

It's for everyone who felt all the anxiety and stress of the world in the days, weeks, months, and years following the U.S. debut of COVID-19 in March 2020. It was, and still is, a scary time, and a large part of this book is about how I learned to cope, survive day-to-day, and eventually grow into a better version of myself. I think you'll find that for all the terrors, bumps, and bruises of those years, all of us grew in some way.

And finally, this book is for all the kids who had to find their own ways to muddle through those bizarre times. In the depths of my own fears and anxiety, I admired the resilience, strength, and flexibility of my kids and others like them who had part of their childhood stripped away in the face of a deadly virus. And making matters worse, they had to watch grownups argue and fight over every issue imaginable, as matters of public health became political punching bags and families and communities were torn apart.

During the pandemic, I held close the hope that humanity would emerge from these difficult times into a better place. More understanding, more loving, less selfish, and more focused on the common good. Believe it or not, I still have that hope. We are certainly not there yet, but sometimes you have to take a step back to move forward.

To all who battled through the years 2020 and 2021, doing your best to keep yourself and those you love safe and sane, this book is for you. I hope you find some resonance and connection in the stories here.

Cheers, and thanks for coming over.

CHAPTER 1

PARENTING, PRODUCTIVITY, AND QUARANTINE

"School Closure Information/Extended Spring Break: Please check your email for district communication, visit their website, or find them on Facebook for the most up-to-date information. We will be closed for extended spring break beginning Monday, March 16."
—Email from the local elementary school (March 11, 2020)

On that first day of the "extended spring break," I started writing a daily blog called "P's and Q̲: Parenting, Productivity, and Quarantine." At the time, I didn't really know what I was doing with it, besides seeing it as a way to write through feelings about what was going on, and maybe share a common experience with other parents going through similar things.

I assumed it would last a few weeks, since I hadn't fully grasped what a long-ranging problem COVID-19 would become. Also, I didn't expect I would be able to stick with the daily routine of posting for very long.

I wound up being wrong on both fronts. The pandemic went on. There were waves of outbreaks with lulls from time to time. It stuck with us and will stick with us for many years. I also far outlived my expectations for writing the blog. I exceeded my initial goal of a few weeks—I posted daily for 450 consecutive days.

During that time, my family and our society experienced an incredible amount of stress, confusion, isolation, and anxiety. It tested each one of us in different ways. We all had to adapt to a brand-new reality that none of us asked for.

It was a traumatic time for everyone, and each of us had our own obstacles to face. For parents, there was the added layer of keeping our children calm and sane through truly unprecedented times. With schools closed and all the usual outlets gone, we were left to our own devices. It felt like we had to make lemonade—not from lemons, but from rocks and old bananas.

What I didn't expect when I started writing the blog, but realized a few months later, was that I was creating a contemporaneous record about the pandemic—a snapshot—and what it was like to be a parent and a human being during that time. At times, I wondered if I could create a book out of my blogged life, but for a long time I didn't really know what that would look like or mean.

My daily blog ended in June 2021. My last post came right after I had become fully vaccinated and took my first work trip since before the pandemic. That felt like a big turning point, returning to the life before. I knew COVID wasn't "over," but it felt like we were shifting into a new phase and it was the right time to move on.

Of course, COVID didn't move on. We had spikes again in the fall, followed by the crushing onslaught of Omicron, where just about everyone seemed to be getting sick. Even if I wasn't writing about life in the pandemic anymore, we were still living some version of it. It didn't take me long to realize that there would be no going back to the time before. Whatever "normal" ultimately looked like would be different.

Almost immediately after finishing the blog, I began writing this book. At first, I viewed the project as some kind of chronicle or history of the pandemic, drawing heavily on the story our family lived during that time. Something about it wasn't feeling right, and I soon realized that I hadn't had enough separation from it all yet.

Still, I kept trying different approaches and started three or four versions of this book before I settled into the lane that landed me here. I struggled a little along the way with tone and purpose. Should the book be a serious examination of the experiences and impacts of that time? Should it be a collection of pandemic-related knock-knock jokes? Or should we look at the reality of that time at all? Certainly there is a strong sentiment in many of us refusing to look back on that time—instead, just kind of forgetting about it and moving on.

Moving on is something I am generally in favor of, in most cases. I agree there is little sense stewing in old emotions from times of crisis, but I also believe that all of us, no matter our situation, experienced trauma. Everyone faced different individual challenges that were either created by or amplified by COVID. Whatever each person's or each family's experience was, I think it's important to acknowledge that we all went through something during that time. We all had to do our best to deal with universally difficult circumstances.

I am someone who believes there are always lessons to be learned from any situation. I learned so much in the time covered in this book. I can honestly say I am not the same person today that I was when shutdowns began in March 2020. Many reading this might feel the same way.

I am something of a nerd and often find parallels in life to quintessential geek culture. One such example is the storytelling vehicle of the long-running British TV series, *Doctor Who*. Since the show has been on for decades, many different actors and actresses have played the role of the Doctor. The gimmick the show uses to explain this is that the Doctor, who lives for thousands of years, regenerates from time to time. Each time the Doctor regenerates, he or she simultaneously becomes a "new" person while still being the same person. At their core, the Doctor is a continuous entity, but each regeneration brings new faces, quirks, and foibles.

For years, I have looked at different periods of my life as my own versions of the Doctor's regenerations. I am still Jim Schneider, the same person, but with fundamental changes. It's how I can look back on myself in my mid-twenties or early thirties and think *Yup, that was me, but a whole different version.*

OK, I am not *something* of a nerd. I **am** a nerd.

In any case, I've had at least ten regenerations since college, and probably two since March of 2020. I think that's a good thing. I think it's good to evolve and change as conditions push us to. Staying the same while so much around us is rapidly changing feels like arrested development.

What I am trying to do with this book is look back on moments my family experienced during the pandemic, and how battling through challenges—related to COVID and those not related to COVID—helped shape us as a family and me as a person. I think being a parent is a process of continuous improvement. Any parent who claims they have it all figured out will get a dubious look from me. I'm a firm believer that on our best days, most parents are just trying to stay afloat and do the best they can.

But I did learn a lot about being a parent from our time together during COVID. And I hope readers find it helpful to share some of those lessons and experiences.

I have drawn on some of my posts or things I wrote in the blog as a way to travel back in time. Another goal with this book is to encourage others to take a gentle look back themselves, in hopes of processing what that time meant and where it led us. It can be unhealthy to simply memory-hole things that we didn't like along our path. It's important to look back on the pandemic years because there is a lot we can learn from them. I hope the stories and essays here offer something relatable to parents or anyone else who is reading. Everyone's experience was different. I don't claim to be an everyman, but maybe a "manyman" at least.

I am a pretty regular guy. Even my name, Jim Schneider, is so common that I was one of two Jim Schneiders growing up in my 3,000-person hometown. Just a few years ago, when I was boarding a plane, I was paged to the gate agent because there was another Jim Schneider on the same flight. They needed to make sure that we were, in fact, two separate people.

Like so many people, I grew up on a small farm near a small town in Wisconsin. My first job in high school was as a disc jockey for a polka radio station. I've lived in California, Chicago, and currently Denver, where I run a regional trade association for concrete producers.

Pretty typical, right? OK, maybe not the polka thing or the concrete thing, but both are 100 percent true. And fear not, this will be the last reference to polka music or concrete you will see in this book. Probably.

I've been a writer for many years, mostly for magazines. Words are a way for me to process information and learn, and one of my favorite things about writing for magazines is that I get to absorb new information. In crafting it to help teach others, I learn so much myself. Even if I didn't really recognize it at the time, writing my blog was a big part of how I processed what I was going through and what our family was going through. It was a difficult, but also surprisingly rewarding, couple of years.

I should make a quick introduction to the cast of characters that will appear throughout the book:

Jim. That's me. Former polka DJ (I didn't *promise* that would be the last reference, did I?), parent, writer, and director of a concrete trade association. I am in many ways a big kid who watches cartoons, appreciates cool toys, enjoys make-believe and playgrounds almost as much as my kids do, and fights my daughter for the last bowl of Count Chocula cereal every October.

Erin. Wife, parent, entrepreneur, coach, and all-around fantastic human being. We've been married since 2009, and I couldn't ask for a better partner in life. She is an amazing mom, a savvy business-woman, and my favorite person. Before COVID, she had been in business as a dog trainer for several years and was in the process of launching a health coaching business in 2020 before the pandemic hit and forced her to step back from it. But she discovered a brand-new path along the way and today works as a parent coach supporting families of neurodiverse children.

Amelia. Daughter, sister, friend, leader, and a smart and genuine spark of a girl. Think of a smile that makes everyone feel good, distilled into human form: that's Amelia. Amelia is one of those people who lights up a room when she walks in. She is positive, gregarious, kind beyond description, curious, creative, clever, a leader, and just a delight to be around.

I know she will do great things because she already does great things. She was seven years old and at the tail end of first grade when the pandemic struck. Amelia loves people and adored her classmates and teacher, which made the shift to remote school a challenge for her—but one she handled with amazing resilience.

Henry. Son, brother, comedian, director, and a dynamic force of brilliance, power, and will. Henry had just turned four when the pandemic started. Of all of us, he may have had the most dramatic regeneration during this time. Henry has always been our jokester. He is hilarious, bright, energetic, and full of confidence. We always say he will absolutely be a CEO  someday because he knows what he wants and makes everyone around him feel like they want the same thing.

Our kids are both amazing, and I am beyond thankful for the time I got to spend with them through the pandemic. They both taught me so much, and still do. One of the themes I discuss in this book is the difference between the early days of COVID, when we seemed focused on the pandemic alone, and the later days when we were juggling so much more. Life marched on, with every individual and family soon realizing that we'd have to deal with COVID alongside the usual parts of life—its normal issues and pitfalls.

The big one for us was that in April of 2020, Henry was diagnosed as being autistic*. It created a fundamental change in our path. To be clear, it doesn't and didn't change who Henry is. This has been part of who he is since he was born, and receiving that understanding just helped us better understand who he is and how we can support him.

Learning this set us on a path of finding help for Henry, learning about neurodiversity, and forging a new way forward. It was scary and confusing in those early days, and it felt like so much on top of COVID. But being able to look back on it now, I am so thankful for Henry's assessment because it allowed us to understand our son's mechanisms and emotions and work hard on building a smoother road forward for him and others like him.

I'll also mention our menagerie of pets: Asta, Islay (pronounced "EYE-luh"), and Maisie. Asta and Islay are both Norfolk terriers, and they are sisters from different litters. We brought home Asta in July of 2019, pre-pandemic, and Islay joined the family on Thanksgiving 2020. And because two loud terriers didn't provide enough insanity for us, we also added Maisie the cat, a rescue, in July of 2021.

So that's a bit about me. And about us. Together, we muddled our way through bizarre, unprecedented times. It was wild, wacky, and sometimes scary, and hard. But I honestly couldn't have asked for a better crew to quarantine with.

Parenting is always an act of improv and attitude in the face of chaos, and this strange period was no different. No matter where you were or who you are, all we parents had to make things up as we went along, and do our best to stay positive in spite of it all.

It was the same for our kids. They had to suddenly contend with an utterly changed world. Many of the things, people, and places they loved were now off-limits. They had lots of time on their hands and the kids, too, required some improv. My two kids had to make their own absurd, creative, wonderful fun—emanating their own light in the darkness, which they taught me a great deal about throughout 2020 and 2021.

This book is a collection of stories, moments, and lessons I learned during our family's particular journey through the pandemic. I wrote daily about our experiences and what I was discovering from March 2020 through June 2021. My daily posts provided me a direct gateway of insight to what we were going through, one that would be lost had I not written things down.

We all went through a lot during those times, and everyone's journey was unique. Frankly, we all have some processing and recovering to do from what were extremely traumatic times. But if my path has taught me anything, it's that there is always something good to be found, even in the toughest of conditions. Growth is always there if we look for it.

I hope sharing my family's story will help others find their own understanding of their own experience. Better still, I hope our story will inspire others to find the wonder, the adventure, and the growth in their own day-to-day family lives.

In my life, I've been fortunate to have some great teachers, and none so great as my own children, Amelia and Henry, and my wife, Erin. I am thankful to be on this wild ride with them. And as with all teachers I've had before, I hope they are grading on a curve.

*A NOTE ABOUT TERMINOLOGY.

There are two general models to refer to individuals with disabilities: identity first and person first. You'll notice throughout the book that we refer to Henry as being an "autistic child" as opposed to "a child with autism." This is an example of identity first, rather than person first language. It is a matter of individual preference in the autistic community, with some people preferring identity first (i.e., autistic person) and others preferring person first (i.e. person with autism). It's always best to ask the person in question what they prefer. In our family, we tend toward identity first as our experience has shown preference in that direction, so you'll see me refer to Henry as "autistic." If you want to learn more about this topic, a great resource is the Autistic Self Advocacy Network (ASAN), which you can visit online at autisticadvocacy.org.

EXCERPT FROM JIM'S ABANDONED BOOK OF COVID KNOCK-KNOCK JOKES

Knock knock!

Who's there?

COVID-19

COVID-19 who?

Just regular old COVID-19. You're exposed! Now don't answer any knocks for two weeks after your last symptoms present, because you're in quarantine.

CHAPTER 2

THE BEFORE TIMES: GOING VIRAL

Ironically, one of the last memories I have of doing things out in the world, in public spaces with other human beings—the "Before Times" that preceded COVID—involved my family getting sick with . . . a virus.

Not the coronavirus, I should note. In fact, I don't know the name of the virus that took us down—it never took the time to extend us the courtesy of introducing itself. I'll call it Zebulon McCranahan, because that is a terrible name that is not easy on the ears, in ways that this virus was not easy on the stomach.

It was early February 2020, a year that we had a booked trip to Hawaii in March. Erin set the launch of her brand-new health coaching business, I was in the early stages of building a budding new podcast and media initiative, and an assortment of other fun was on the docket. Things were looking up! The Schneider family was going to OWN the year 2020.

Or it was going to own us. One or the other.

We had big plans to go out for my wife's birthday on February 2. I had booked us a spot at Punchbowl Social, this fun place with games, bowling, and the whole celebratory shebang. We were excited to celebrate, not only because it was my wife's birthday, but because her *previous* birthday we were supposed to go out to dinner and have a night out on the town . . . but a stomach bug took us all out. What a bummer. I had sure hoped that wouldn't happen again.

Birthday 2020's festivities started with us arriving at Punchbowl Social and discovering that our reservations were, in fact, for the *other* location in Denver, which was on the other side of town. I was mortified at my planning gaffe and stumbled around trying to figure out what to do. Turned out, we could get a table where we were in maybe fifteen minutes, so it wasn't worth schlepping around.

Erin took it in stride, but I was feeling pretty bad about the goof. Pretty soon, we were at a table and all was good. Drinks were ordered, including big, over-the-top milkshakes festooned with sparklers.

Around the appetizer course was when I started to feel a little rumbly in the tummy, but I shrugged it off. *I can't possibly get sick two years in a row, right?*

I muddled through dinner, feeling worse and worse, but putting on my best face. It wasn't working all that well and my wife saw through it. But I insisted that maybe dinner wasn't agreeing with me.

And to be fair, that was a possibility. Was it hubris on my part, on the year anniversary of being sick to my stomach on my wife's birthday, to order lobster nachos at a restaurant approximately 2,000 miles away from the nearest seafood-providing coast? That's possible. Both lobster and nachos on their own aren't well known for their stomach-soothing properties. Put it all together and I may have been playing a real game of digestive roulette here.

As soon as my son was done eating, I took it as the perfect excuse to usher Henry outside to run around and let off steam. Henry is not big on sitting still, and nothing in my stomach was interested in sitting still at this moment either.

Amelia joined us, and the fresh air was helping me a little. The kids romped around, making their own fun just running back and forth, as they often do. I was in that zone where I'd have a few minutes feeling like *Yeah, I'm just fine*, followed by a couple minutes of wanting to double over on the ground.

After playing some games with the kids, we decided it was time to head back to Erin's parents' house for cake and presents. I was keeping it together, but it was getting harder to grin through my nausea. Time came to open presents, and the gift I bought Erin that year was tickets to see David Gray, her favorite artist, at the Greek Theater in Los Angeles. We were going to take a trip to Los Angeles that summer and pack in with a bunch of other fans for the White Ladder 20th Anniversary Tour.

The tickets to the LA show meant another fun trip for us to take, and also a chance for Erin to see the concert she *so* wanted to see. Win, win, win. I just threw in that third "win" because it was so much winning. I could have probably gone with a fourth, but I try to practice economy in writing.

After my proud victory lap of a gift well received, my stomach twisted into some kind of sailor's knot, and I could no longer deny that I was feeling awful. Still thinking it was food poisoning or something like it, we went home and I went to bed. It was a super rough night, to say the least, and I don't need to go into any further detail than that.

I felt awful in the morning, and it turned out that now the birthday girl did, too. Soon the kids would follow, and this stomach bug would ravage the house, as it had the year before. How dare a tiny virus ruin our fun like this! In the year 2020? It seemed inconceivable. I mean, it's supposed to be the year of winning!

In addition, Erin and I were set to go to Las Vegas in a couple of days. It was a work trip for me, but Erin was going to come along and hang out with some other friends of ours there.

We thought about cancelling but in a couple days were feeling well enough to go. However, in Las Vegas, we were both still limping off the remnants of that stomach bug. We'd go out to dinner but not really have an appetite. Suffice to say, we didn't whoop it up very much. We got out a little, but certainly not as much as one might have liked to have if one would have known one was standing on the precipice of a multiyear pandemic that would have everyone housebound for a year.

Reflecting on the Punchbowl Puke-O-Rama and the half-effort Las Vegas trip seems very strange now. It all took place about a month and a half before the full COVID shutdown happened in March of 2020. It feels like that was the last dash of Before Times—normal life before the world changed completely. It was also kind of a funny sample section of what was supposed to be an action-packed, winning year filled with fun and travel. Even before COVID, this big birthday party and travel adventure was all tainted by a virus.

Just not THE virus.

By then we had certainly been made aware of COVID-19. It was still this kind of freaky thing happening a world away. There were rumbles of concern that it could reach here, but still no real conception of what that would mean. I remember in Las Vegas, sitting out on my room's balcony texting some doctor friends, and we were joking about being sure to stay away from the virus. The idea that it could be out there existed, but we weren't taking it seriously.

Months into the lockdown, a video from that night at the Puke-O-Rama birthday outing came up on my phone, catching my attention. It haunted me. It was a moment I had forgotten about entirely in all the fast-moving craziness of the spring of 2020.

In the video, the kids were running around at dusk, dancing and rocking out to some excellent classic punk playing on the loudspeakers. They were jamming out in a fun, frolicky dance in magic-hour light right in front of big letters spelling out "DENVER."

Until I saw the video, I had forgotten about it all. But apparently, even though I was feeling the ravages of a stomach bug that night, I must have thought this was a moment worth capturing. Something must have told me that moment was special. And it was. In many ways, it was one of the last moments of pure expression and joy before the whole world changed. The trips to Hawaii and Los Angeles, as well as a long list of plans, hopes and dreams got swallowed up by the pandemic. Our path, like the paths of people and families all around the world, changed on a dime.

That doesn't mean that there weren't beautiful moments during the pandemic. It just meant they were different, and we were on a different timeline, a different path. In a few weeks, when we were confined to our homes and I was writing a daily blog, I found myself finding those kinds of moments and recording them every single day. I started the daily blog, at first as just something to do, and eventually it became a challenge designed to expand my writing horizons, and a way to cope with life around us.

In the height of the pandemic, when I would look back at those events—the birthday, the trip, the dancing—I had felt an overwhelming loss of what was in the time before and was supposed to be on that timeline we never got to explore. But when I look at it all in totality now, I see that even that birthday, that moment, was far from perfect.

It's a bit ironic to me that we all got sick before the world got sick and stopped. And then, being confined to our house and taking all the precautions, none of us really got sick at all for about a year. And even things like taking Henry outside to run around that night of the birthday outing, that was part of our coping to deal with the fact that he would melt down if he had to be at the table too long.

Any time we went out, I wound up chasing Henry around for most of the time. It was something we didn't recognize or have any grasp on then, but later would learn a lot more about after he was identified as autistic.

The Before Time is easy to look at through rose-colored glasses and lament all the things that could have been. Those trips to Hawaii and Los Angeles, as well as the businesses we thought we'd be starting . . . none of those happened. But other good things did, and we wound up on the path we were supposed to be on instead.

But if I did carry any lesson through from the Before Time, it's that lobster nachos are probably never a good idea.

DO YOU REMEMBER?

Harry and Meghan? In January of 2020, in the fading weeks of the Before Time, England's Prince Harry and Meghan Markle announced they were stepping back from their royal duties.

The news sent shockwaves around the world at the time, but in retrospect, they were simply a little ahead of what would become a very prominent COVID-era trend of people working remotely and reinventing their jobs entirely.

CHAPTER 3

LOFT-Y EXPECTATIONS

The early days of the COVID pandemic were horrifying, but also oddly peaceful.

As a person who has long lived his life riddled with anxiety about a lot of things—work, finances, family, politics, climate change, the fact that I'm the only person I know who hasn't watched *Breaking Bad*—there was something nice about having just one, singular, powerful burning point of terror to focus on. In a way, it was actually kind of soothing.

It really weeded out a lot of that other stuff for a while, the usual stuff I worried about, and instead let me focus on whether or not I touched my face while shopping at Trader Joe's and whether or not I'd ever be able to find a bottle of hand sanitizer on a store shelf ever again.

Still, at the beginning, it felt like a very temporary thing because, of course, all bad things are temporary. As a society, we haven't dealt with a sprawling, long-running national tragedy since *According to Jim* kept getting renewed, year after year . . . for eight seasons.

So, when the whole pandemic thing first hit, I found myself in something of a focused, Zen state. I no longer worried about what was going to happen months from now. I was very zeroed-in on the moment and finding our way as a family through unprecedented times.

When lockdown started, I joined legions of parents all around the country suddenly finding themselves in close working quarters with their kids. What could go wrong?

Well, as we all found out . . . pretty much anything and everything could go wrong. Things like focus, privacy, and professional decorum pretty much go out the window when you're cleaning Cheetos crumbs off your desk and trying to make phone calls between the screams of bored and hungry children.

My office is in a loft in our house, which most times is awesome. Lots of light, nice and open—it's a really nice workspace. What it lacks, of course, is walls.

Walls can be helpful, as it turns out. Walls prevent one's young son from barging in and demanding to know what's for dinner . . . at 10 a.m.

Now, I should say that working at home with kids around is not something new for me. I'd been working out of a home office for about five years when COVID came around, and I had gotten used to juggling work and kids for some time. But there was always some kind of safety net, whether that was having them gone for a few hours at school or day care, having a babysitter in the house, or some other means of distraction. Now, the net was gone. And we were all in freefall.

The very first day of the kids being home from school was the day I decided to start writing a daily blog about the pandemic quarantine experience. And the very first picture I used in that first post summed up much of the experience for me: It was me in my living room chair with my laptop, looking haggard, with Henry right next to me crying.

Honestly, that morning had gone surprisingly well. The kids were getting along. Sure, I had a few work distractions, but nothing awful. Things seemed to be proceeding somewhat peacefully. I even remember saying out loud, "Maybe this won't be so bad after all."

I don't have many deep spiritual beliefs in specific gods or other deities. I instead subscribe much more to the concept of a universal current or energy. That said, I absolutely believe in the existence of some kind of Jinx god or Jinx force. In this case, I very strongly and definitely taunted that god, and soon found myself smote.

"This won't be so bad after all" is exactly the phrase any Jinx god waits for, and whereupon smiles and says, "It. Is. Done."

The delicate peace lasted until right around lunchtime, and by early afternoon, the wheels had completely come off the quarantine vehicle. The kids were bickering, and when they weren't arguing over who gets to watch what on TV, they were nagging me for snacks, complaining about boredom, and on and on and on. The rest of the day was a chaotic, senseless disaster, much like any given episode of *According to Jim*.

The interruptions were constant. As any parent will tell you, kids asking for snacks are RELENTLESS. It's seriously like the old gag of someone saying, "How about now? Now? Now? What about now?" Trying to stop it is like trying to ward off a tsunami with a kid's plastic beach bucket.

With no more than eight seconds between food requests, trying to work became nothing short of maddening. I will readily admit to caving quickly to snack requests so many times during COVID. Like throwing a steak at hungry dogs to keep them off your heels, I would have to throw Goldfish crackers or potato chips at my kids to allow me at least a few quiet moments to do my job and take a breath.

Henry was getting crankier and more demanding as the day went on, and he really wanted to sit next to me. I was OK with that, as he was just watching *Bubble Guppies* or something. The trouble was that Henry, a kid with heightened sensory needs, insisted on holding my hand.

That's adorable if nothing else is going on and you're just looking to cuddle and watch TV. But try typing emails with an extremely determined (and strong) four-year-old clutching your left hand. Yeah, it's not super easy.

I argued with him and tried to pull my hand away, explaining I needed it to type. He kept saying "It's MY HAND!" Not to be argumentative or contrary, but here was the point where I had to agree to disagree. While I am someone who tries very hard to see other peoples' point of view, in this case, I was pretty sure this hand had been connected to my wrist for some forty-six years. And I was pretty sure that this fact of biology and physics implies ownership. I didn't have documents or anything, but still.

The whole thing devolved to Henry crying and fake moaning with a pained soullessness that could only be compared to the hollow, tinny sounds of the laugh track on an episode of *According to Jim*.

Later, the kids were playing outside. Thinking I had earned a moment of respite from the madness, I instead heard screaming and discovered my son had covered himself in dirt and leaves like some kind of feral boy-beast from *Lord of the Flies*. But he smiled and laughed all the way through the dust and filth, so in the end, at least he was happy.

That first week or two was a very chaotic repetition of this pattern. Not only were Erin and I trying to figure out how to keep the kids entertained and sane in this scary and weird time, I was also trying to figure out how my job would work. In the early days, it was a little like Wile E. Coyote, still running even though he was floating several feet off the cliff and gravity just hadn't kicked in yet.

My job was going to change radically in the coming months, but at this point, I was still doing all the usual stuff, like everything was going to be totally back to normal in just a few weeks. I was postponing trips and office visits by just a few weeks, because come on, how long could this last?

Without going into the gory details, my job as the director of a small regional trade association meant that a lot of what I do is go out and visit the offices of architects and engineers, give presentations, and teach people about cool things you can do with concrete. The job involved some travel, setting up meetings, and lots of things that involve human interaction.

As it became increasingly clear that this wasn't going anywhere for a while, I had to face the reality that I was going to have to find other ways to accomplish the goals of the job—and do it in ways that didn't involve my leaving the house.

There certainly were a few weeks where I flailed around a little with that. *What is this "Zoom" thing and can I somehow use it to give presentations? I wonder.*

I was scared, as many were, about what was going on in the world and couldn't help but wonder what that would mean for my own employment situation and my family. It was stressful, and it weighed heavy on me.

As correspondence started slowing down and the world retreated into a bit of a cocoon, I settled into a pretty distinct funk for a few weeks. It was a low-energy, high-depression zone.

It was affecting all of us and forcing adjustments all around. When lockdown hit, Erin was just a few weeks into the launch of a new business venture, offering health coaching services to postpartum women. It was something she had long wanted to do, and she had spent the previous year studying and completing an intensive certification course. She was networking, developing content, and building a voice on social media when everything just abruptly stopped.

Like me, in the first few weeks, she was working on things and treating the COVID lockdown as a temporary pause. Erin was also trying to figure out how to move forward during a time life was in stasis.

For the kids, what began as an "extended spring break" soon shifted into a long-term change. Amelia started the early version of virtual school, which was extremely challenging in those opening months. The structure just wasn't there yet, and it was difficult and confusing for kids and parents alike. And for Henry, his time in preschool just stopped. This meant a shattered routine for a boy who thrives on structure. And it meant a sudden goodbye to teachers and classmates he'd known for a couple of years.

We were all in a daze, trying to do "normal" things as the realization set in that normal had gone bye-bye. Sleep was dysregulated. Stress and worry kept me up at night. Henry had been off afternoon naps for a while, but now with his routine shattered too, he suddenly needed them again. So, for a little while, we had kind of a family afternoon naptime. Erin and Henry would go upstairs for quiet time or a little nod off, I'd let Amelia watch cartoons, and I'd pop in my earbuds and take a quick afternoon nap on the sofa.

I felt so guilty about taking those thirty-minute naps. It was daytime and I was *supposed* to be working. Sure, most of the people I normally interact with weren't in their offices, the world was shut down, many folks were curled in a fetal position on the floor, and very little business was happening, but still! We have this inherent feeling that our time and our lives belong to someone else during those daytime hours. Taking little naps made me feel like I was no different than George Costanza sneaking naps under his desk on *Seinfeld*.

None of us was doing much sleeping at night in those first few months. Kids were attuned to and nervous about all the uncertainty, which meant Amelia and Henry were having more bad dreams and restless nights, too. Many nights were spent with one kid in our bed with Erin, and the other in the guest bed with me. They were scared about how much their lives had changed. And frankly, so was I.

With all that happened, it's important for me to recognize that those naps back then really helped me get back on track and start getting things done again. It was a small thing, but this was an example of COVID teaching me a little something about priorities. And as time wore on, I kept having to learn and relearn the lesson that my mental health and well-being was important, too.

My crisis response is generally to feel like I always need to be doing something. Always vigilant. When it became clear the pandemic wasn't going to be a short-term thing, I had to wake up to the fact that this was a marathon, not a race, and that maybe, just maybe, I needed to have more realistic expectations for myself.

Taking those thirty-minute catnaps wasn't hurting anyone, and it sure was helping me. The second part of that equation—helping *me*—is a fairly basic concept that I still grapple with, and I know lots of other parents do, too. But it is important and necessary. Pandemic or not, parenting is hard, life is wacky, and it is super important to understand this big idea: taking care of ourselves doesn't mean we're taking any less care of anyone else.

DO YOU REMEMBER?

A call for global unity on COVID? On March 23, 2020, United Nations Secretary General António Guterres called for an immediate global ceasefire amid the pandemic to "fight the common enemy."

And the rest was history. Peace was declared worldwide and humanity came together to fight the coronavirus together. The pandemic was eventually defeated when Iron Man tricked the virus into relinquishing all six Infinity Stones.

CHAPTER 4

I HATE THIS COLD!

For at least the first few months of the pandemic, our universe shrunk immensely. It was basically the walls of our house and our modest little fenced-in backyard.

There was some part of me that found comfort in the security of that. Like a weighted blanket or how a baby likes to be swaddled. But having two kids used to going out on lots of adventures to parks, playgrounds, and indoor activity areas made the sudden strict limitations more challenging.

The panic and confusion of parents in the first weeks and months of the pandemic was universal. I know parents everywhere were experiencing it. We may have all had different situations and nuance, but one thing unified us all: what in the world were we going to do with these kids all day, every day?

All the usual outlets and tricks were suddenly gone. For those of us who relied on school or day care to occupy our kids for a few hours each day so we could get other things done, that was gone in a snap.

But it went farther than that. Even if you were a parent with your kids at home already, suddenly there were no playgrounds, no children's museums, no out-of-the-house activities of any kind.

We have three playgrounds within walking distance of our house, and in the Before Times, I would take the kids to any one of them several times a week, just to give them a change of scenery and let them run around. We also have a great little children's museum nearby that we enjoyed so much that we decided to invest in an annual membership in January 2020. I would take the kids there at least twice a month, and I remembered figuring that if I just took them there five times all year, we'd be ahead on the annual membership.

By the middle of March, when the world shut down, I had taken them there four times. Missed it by THAT much.

During the early weeks of shutdown, I saw a flurry of social media posts from fellow parents suggesting cool activities and projects to keep kids busy and entertained so they wouldn't go insane and drag us down with them. There were virtual museum tours, tons of structured activities, and ideas for fun things to do in quarantine. It seemed like a whole cottage industry of household fun blew up early on, and then by May, most parents were way too exhausted to keep up with any of it.

And beyond the surface layer of keeping kids busy and entertained, there was the deeper issue of finding ways to talk to them about what was going on. At ages seven and four, our kids were just old enough to kind of understand something was happening, but not necessarily sophisticated enough to understand why it meant they couldn't go to a McDonald's PlayPlace or have their friends come over.

After a few weeks, when the novelty of having extra time off from school had worn off, both kids really began to chafe. Henry was bouncing off the walls and having more meltdowns. Even the usually positive and ebullient Amelia was cranky and angry. Once, she came stamping down the stairs, her brow furrowed in frustration.

"Dad, I want to go to the children's museum," she ordered.

"It's closed honey, I'm sorry. We can't."

"Why is it still closed?"

"You know why, Amelia. It's because of the cold."

When talking to the kids about the pandemic in the early days, we called COVID "the cold." It just felt like the best way to explain it to them at the time. Even we grown-ups only had the roughest idea of what it was back then, so trying to turn around and explain basic virology and epidemiology to a seven-year-old and a four-year-old seemed like a super heavy lift.

"Hey kids, let's talk about viruses! Now a virus is something really, really tiny."

"Like an M&M?"

"No, quite a bit smaller than that."

"Like half an M&M?"

"No, more like so small you can't even see it."

"They can turn invisible?!"

"Um, sure. Anyway, they're both everywhere and nowhere, and they're going to upend your life for a couple years."

Like many heavy issues and questions, I would fall into the tried-and-true parental approach of postponing any kind of real answer. "It's a really bad cold that people are nervous about," was the best dodge I could conjure, and at least was something relatable the kids could understand.

And to be fair, I think in the opening weeks of the pandemic, there was still this naïve feeling that it would pass in short order, and we wouldn't have to go into deeper explanation. At the time, I thought I was being the sober realist by thinking *Boy, these folks who think the pandemic will pass by the end of April are being a little overly optimistic. I'm betting more like June.*

Of course, June of *which* year was the real question.

But back to the stairway conversation.

Amelia flopped down on the stairs, and asked with great exasperation, "When is this cold going to go away?"

"I really don't know Amelia," I said. This came out with a quiet tone of defeat that was maybe among the first moments that I realized I couldn't put a positive spin on this one.

My daughter, a very chipper and positive person, seldom prone to loud bursts of frustration or anger, threw up her hands and shouted to the heavens, "I HATE THIS COLD!"

"We all do," was all I could say back.

We both shared in a moment of sadness, fear, and frustration and hugged.

It could be that one of the hardest lessons I had to learn during the pandemic—and I should note, this one I had to learn over and over and over again—is that there are just times we can't do anything for our kids other than be there. It is a lousy and helpless feeling because we always want to solve the problem, but sometimes we have to just coach our kids through times when life is difficult.

Amelia and Henry had a right to feel angry and sad and frustrated by the fact that so many of the things they used to love doing, we just couldn't do. Those feelings would bubble to the surface sometimes, and I admit, after that interaction, I worried a lot about how the kids would handle things over however long this reality would exist.

In all the different stages of the pandemic, we tried to find joy and create special moments whenever and however we could. It helped keep the kids' spirits up and made it so at least every day wasn't exactly the same as the last. The monotony can really bring you down, and we tried hard to avoid falling into that trap.

Sometimes, when we were lucky, there were small things that just organically were special. In April 2020, the movie *Trolls World Tour* became one of the first major productions to account for the pandemic lockdown and debut on a digital format, so people could watch at home. Our kids love the original *Trolls* movie, so we treated it like a major premiere in our house. We had a pizza night and rented the movie the night it came out.

We all grinned and laughed watching it the first time. The movie was good, sure. But as much as anything, it was a refreshing contrast to the darkness of the world we were living in at the time. The cheery, fun music and upbeat vibe provided us a truly uplifting, positive escape.

The kids *loved* the movie, and the big problem was that the rental lasted for only two days. They watched it nonstop for those two days. I remember how sad they were when I told them on Sunday night that it would be the end of the rental. "We'll buy it when it comes out," I assured them. "Don't worry!"

But they loved the songs so much. The last night of that rental, I sat in bed with the kids and we all sang along to "Just Sing," the song at the end of the movie. It is a moment that still stays with me and ignites a big warm spot inside.

The next day we were back to the grind, the kids depressed that the movie was gone. Big softy that I am, I'll fully admit that I relented and rented it again. And again. And again. When all was said and done, I'm somewhat ashamed to say we spent over $100 *renting* this movie. So, congratulations, movie studio people. You won. I'm a sucker.

Expense aside, the story has a happy ending. To this day, that movie and its music bring a smile to my face, and it does still get regularly watched in our house. Yes, I did stick to my promise of buying the movie for real when it became available. And the good news, dear reader, is that having rented the movie gave me a TEN PERCENT discount on the eventual purchase of the film on iTunes.

Yes, I may have spent a hundred dollars renting the movie, but it did ultimately save me like a buck-ninety when I purchased it to own. Checkmate! Who's the sucker now, movie studio people? Yeah, you know it.

DO YOU REMEMBER?

Defunding the World Health Organization? On April 14, 2020, President Donald Trump announced halting funding to WHO, because of China or something. It was an excellent strategic move to further starve the organization best positioned to actually help.

This follows the less formal defunding of The Who, a band who hasn't been culturally relevant for several decades.

CHAPTER 5

FENCEBAT

When I was growing up, my siblings and I used to make up a lot of crazy games and come up with lots of silly ways to pass the time. It was no different for Amelia and Henry living through pandemic lockdown.

To counter the fear and gloom of the outside world, we worked hard to generate a little positivity bubble in our home. This is where the kids' creativity and imagination came in very handy, and we leaned heavily into that. We did our best to make the biggest world out of the space our home provided us. The house itself became many things: a castle, a spaceship, and a series of other planets.

We would designate certain days as kind of made-up holidays. Amelia was integral in this process. We would have dress-up day or celebrate the pretend birthday of some stuffy or toy. Sometimes we'd even mark these occasions by making a cake, singing songs, or having a "party," which basically resembled a slightly more festive version of our regular dinner—but with cake.

Boxes bearing delivery items to our house were transformed into cars, planes, boats, and spaceships. Our basement became a hangar for an impressive fleet of box vehicles that grew and grew as the pandemic went on. We invented lots of backyard games with random toys and unmatching sports equipment.

We would play imaginary games, like shopping, where the kids would set up little "stores" that Erin and I would take turns visiting to peruse their wares. These games usually started off pretty traditional, but then would transform into unexpected bits of make-believe fusion. One of my favorite examples was that the kids liked to play restaurant, where they'd take our orders and bring us food. They also sometimes liked to play hospital, where I'd come in for very medically intensive examinations of my elbow and hair.

One day, we were playing pizza restaurant, followed by hospital, when one of the kids had the fantastic idea of "Pizza Hospital." I have to say, I am in love with this idea, still. Sure, hospitals aren't always the happiest places for people, but what about a Pizza Hospital? Pizza makes everything better. I can't decide whether it's better to shop this concept around as a sitcom or to actually talk to investors about creating a nationwide chain of pizzeria hospitals.

The kids and I would have fantastical make-believe adventures as superheroes aboard a spaceship. The game would weave in and out of whatever we were doing, whether that was watching a movie or eating a meal. Our house was a big spaceship in this game, and we took it on lots of adventures to places exotic and mundane. But what I really loved about that game was that it would just appear at random moments. I'd be doing something and one of kids would yell out of nowhere, "Turn the ship RIGHT!"

That was my cue to grab an imaginary steering wheel wherever I was standing and make a hard turn, after which the kids would fly to the ground like crew members on the old *Star Trek* series when the USS *Enterprise* would alter course.

This would happen usually when I was cooking, working, cleaning up, or doing whatever around the house, and every time, we would all end up in giggles. The spaceship steering game went on at least into late 2021.

As the weather got nicer in early days of lockdown, the circle of games expanded to the backyard, where several new sports and outdoor activities came to life.

We had a few odds and ends of sports equipment the kids would play with, even before the pandemic. There was a little kiddie basketball hoop, a soccer ball, and a big foam bat with a Nerf softball. I would often pitch the ball to the kids and give them a little batting practice.

One day, I looked out in the backyard and the kids were pitching the ball to each other, playing a little baseball. I was glad to see both of them getting more confident in pitching and went back to whatever I was doing, letting them do their thing.

When I checked in on them later, I saw that what started out as a regular game of baseball turned into something else. I saw the red foam bat sticking out of the lats in the fence and both kids jumping at it, trying to get it out.

I shook my head, laughed, and went out to help them get it out. I often had to go out and help when the ball would go over the fence, but this was a new one. "I don't even want to know how that happened," I chuckled, handing the bat back to Henry before going back inside.

Of course, what I didn't realize was that putting the bat in the fence wasn't a mistake of the game, it *was* the game. They both squealed with joy and went back to jumping and trying to slide the bat back into the fence.

And thus, Fencebat was born.

I know you're asking, *What are the rules of Fencebat?*

I had a similar question when I saw what was going on. But I quickly discovered that asking about the rules of Fencebat is to demonstrate a deep misunderstanding of what Fencebat is.

Fencebat is an expression of chaos in a chaotic world. It's a no-rules framework for kids living through a period that is nothing but walls, limitations, and barriers. It's a lot of CAN in a world of CANNOT.

Top-line: it's jumping up and trying to jam a bat in a fence; it's just plain, silly fun. The bat looks absurd and funny sticking out of the fence, and the kids were in fits of laughter, cracking each other up with their clumsy attempts to get it in there. If Fencebat was scored based on laughter (or if it had any form of scorekeeping, for that matter), all players would be winners anyway.

Fencebat was just one of many, many ways we transformed our backyard into a space where imagination and fun were enhanced and encouraged. There were lots of outdoor dance parties. I've been to dance clubs, Burning Man, and a few raves, but none of them hold a candle to the dance parties in our backyard. And as a middle-aged dad, there is so much joy in dancing with kids who are too young and are having too much fun to understand what a rotten dancer I am. I don't assume *that* will last forever.

In the summer, we rolled out a little backyard sprinkler, which Henry called "the Sprinkerator," a decidedly better name. We also ordered a small inflatable pool and an inflatable rainbow arch sprinkler. By mid-summer, we had an elaborate setup with two sprinklers and the pool at the bottom of the tiny little backyard slide. Presto! The kids had a bona fide pandemic water park of their own. Hot afternoons were spent running and sliding through and into the cool water.

In between games of Fencebat and sprinkler fun, we also played some traditional baseball, and the kids were obsessed with hitting "home runs," which were just knocking the ball over our fence. It meant dad spent a lot of time running into the alley for that home-run ball. But hey, it's all part of the game.

The little slide was on one of those small plastic backyard kiddie forts, which also happened to be near the basketball hoop. Before long, Henry started using it as a jumping platform for all kinds of wacky, Harlem Globetrotters-esque dunks and slams. Between all of this and other games that would burn bright and vanish fast, we had quite a unique, freestyle *Wild World of Sports* going on.

It's hard to know what the long-term effects of the pandemic are going to be like for any of us, both adults and kids. We will all be walking off trauma from it, and it will color our kids' worldview forever. They experienced a time unlike anything we ever had as kids, so it's hard to have a frame of reference for what that will mean.

But if something good can come of it, I hope it's that understanding that no matter what the outside conditions are, and no matter how dark our surroundings might be, it's in our power to create moments of laughter and joy. It doesn't take much, just a little imagination and will.

As a kid growing up in the country, I was in my imagination a lot. Where I was, space wasn't the issue. It was infinite with enormous, wide-open fields all around, a big house and barn, and lots of room to roam. But that can feel lonely and isolating, too. My imagination took me on lots of adventures to other places and worlds I couldn't dream of seeing for real.

Being an adult sometimes makes me feel like I've lost my connection to that world. Growing up means shifting focus more to the "real" world. And sadly, the older I got, the more my overactive imagination started dedicating itself to inventing flights of fancy about things to worry over—a little something doctors like to call "anxiety."

But in moments playing with the kids, even before the pandemic, I felt sparks of connection to that fanciful, imaginative play I used to love when I was their age. Lots of times, I'm tired and it's hard to find the energy to engage in that kind of play when the kids want to, but I always walk away feeling better for having done it.

Fencebat was nothing more than an amusing expression of absurdity and laughter, and a perfect example of how it's possible to conjure fun from literally anything. The game itself is clearly ridiculous, but how much it made the kids laugh is real and meaningful.

That goes for me, too. Weeks after that first Fencebat game, there would be nights when I'd put things away in the yard and see that bat sticking out of the fence. I would laugh every time.

And I loved the places our imaginary spaceship house took us, just as much as kids did. The pandemic was a big reminder of the importance of play and imagination. It deepened my connection with the kids, and it helped keep us all as cheerful and positive as possible during those days. Perhaps most importantly, it was fun. I feel fortunate to be able to look back on the most difficult of times and actually find myself overwhelmed by happy memories.

Writing this now, I'm realizing we haven't had a game of Fencebat in quite a long time. And neither Amelia nor Henry have asked me to steer the ship in a while. Maybe those games finally came to an end, or maybe they're just on a break. As long as I live, I will always be ready to fence that bat or grab that wheel.

EXCERPT FROM JIM'S ABANDONED BOOK OF COVID KNOCK-KNOCK JOKES

Knock knock!
Who's there?
PCR.
PCR who?
PC-are you cool with putting your life on hold and waiting two days for test results? Because that's how long it takes.

CHAPTER 6

HOARD-AK*

The chapter title "Hoard-ak" is a pun of poor quality and nerdy obscurity, even for this author. For those who did not grow up glued to cartoons in the 1980s and/or are not major dorks, the character Hordak, according to Wikipedia is ". . . a fictional character in the Masters of the Universe franchise who opposes She-Ra and He-Man, as well as the franchise's main villain, Skeletor, to whom he was once a mentor, and the cause of the latter's ambition and pursuits of evil." That's right, he sucks so much even the bad guys hate him. The following story discusses the author's pandemic hoarding tendencies, and his near obsessive need to pepper his prose with outdated pop culture references clearly inspired him to reach for this rather pedestrian and obvious play on words. Please continue reading and let's pretend this chapter title never happened.
—Editor

The first few weeks of the pandemic saw unprecedented change in the basic operations of life.

Everyone was struggling to adjust, and parents were overwhelmed with scary questions and brand-new worries.

There were the basic red-alert uncertainties, like *When will my child be able to go back to school? WILL my child be able to go back to school? Will I still have a job when this is all over?* and *What will we do if one of us gets sick?*

But then there were also other more mundane, but equally terrifying, questions like *Where will I be able to find toilet paper?*

Yeah, that was a real and scary thing for a while. We got down-to-the-wire on paper products a couple of times. I also remember being on a months-long quest for any kind of disinfectant wipes or sprays. And randomly, I couldn't find a can of pizza sauce anywhere for almost two months.

I'm sure this kind of thing made everyone nervous. And in my case, it triggered some curious anxious tendencies I'd long forgotten I had. Yup, it turned out I can be a bit of a hoarder.

When the whole thing started and we had no idea what lockdown was going to be like, I went bananas stocking up on everything I could think of (including bananas) because I didn't know when or if I'd be able to get those things again. Particularly that first week or so, I honestly didn't know when or if I'd be able to get back to the store.

I settled eventually into a weekly supply run to limit my time in public. As was suggested back then, we just sent one person (me) to do the shopping. Before COVID, the kids used to come with me grocery shopping quite often. But for much of 2020, I was flying solo.

The experience of going to the store was stressful. Everyone was scared. Everyone was rushing around and probably feeling like I was, asking what they needed to get, in case they wouldn't be back again for a while. And of course, that also meant some of the stuff you were looking for would be cleared out or have limits on how many of those particular items you could take.

For a stretch in March and April of 2020, I'd load up the cart like I was never getting back and was spending an insane amount of money on groceries. Our pantry and freezer were stuffed to capacity. Instead of working through the stockpile we had, I just kept adding to it.

I thought there was at least a chance we'd be locked out of stores for a few weeks. And if that was the case, I should be ready with some emergency rations that would hold up over time. So, I thought *canned goods!* I had a bunch of cans of various beans and things, as well as lots of dry pasta and other things that would last a while.

While I probably wasn't at the official clinical definition of a hoarder, I was definitely hoard-adjacent. I hadn't pushed down any old ladies for a can of black beans or a marble rye. But I was overthinking our supply situation and getting really stressed out about it.

Just before the lockdown, I had tried a pasta recipe that involved cannellini beans and really liked it. Of course, the reality would be that we got a little tired of that dish after a couple times, and since then, I haven't found much application for those hoarded cans I bought.

I was going way overboard on the survivalist stuff. At some point, Erin gently pointed it out to me, and I was overwhelmed with embarrassment and insecurity upon realizing what I was doing. My reaction was filled with defensiveness and shame, and I didn't immediately understand why.

To Erin's immense credit, she calmly talked me through the situation. I think when she brought it up, I was worried that she might be upset by the huge grocery bills or the bursting pantry, but what was really happening was that she saw I was struggling and wanted to offer support and help.

I know none of us is perfect and I am all too human, but this was a deep, dark anxiety expressing itself in ways I wasn't proud of. We talked and she helped me dig in and get to the root of what was pushing me in this direction.

My parents were stocker-uppers. When I was a little kid in the 1980s, I spent a decent amount of time worrying that nuclear war or another disaster was around the corner, and my folks did have a very healthy stockpile of canned food and water, just in case. What I discovered was that my disaster reflex from my childhood had been bubbling up, and I hadn't even noticed.

Once aware of it, I was able to scale back, thankfully. Erin really helped me understand what was happening, and more importantly, to be OK with it—we all have our triggers. This was a stressful time and one of mine had been tripped. It was important for me to see, recognize, and acknowledge my behavior and then work to put it in perspective, rather than run myself down for a tendency I wasn't proud of.

It's not to say that this anxious hoarding voice went away. I was just able to keep that voice in check. I started focusing on trying to work through groceries and other items we already had, with some success. Not perfect, but manageable.

I'm thankful Erin was able to come to me in the spirit of support to help me find my way through it. A few days later, I wrote about this in my blog, which was another big step forward for me. I have traditionally used writing more as a way to hide the parts of me I'm not proud of. So instead, using it to honestly express my struggles was something new. That small step helped me progress further as I wrote the blog for another year.

At the time of this writing, two-and-a-half years after the COVID lockdown struck, several of those cans of cannellini beans remain on my shelf. Throughout the pandemic, they served as a reminder and a reality check for me when my paranoid, survivalist thoughts reemerge. It is also one of the little totems that reminds me of those strange, early days and just how quickly the things we take for granted can change.

I think the hoarding instinct that showed itself in me during those early days indicated a larger issue I have with faith. I don't mean faith in the religious sense; I mean the basic faith that things are going to be OK.

That was something I had to work really hard to come to grips with during the pandemic. No one can live in emergency panic mode forever. And at some point, I had to allow myself to adjust to the new reality and accept some faith that, on a basic survival level, everything was going to be OK.

I had to accept that I would be able to go to the store again the following week without needing to fill up two carts every time I went. I had to accept that we wouldn't run out of food, and that my family would be OK. Those were the starting points I had to work on before I could build to bigger things. When I would feel myself drift, turning to Erin would remind me that I was not in it alone. Sometimes—at least for me—when I'm too locked up in my own head, simply seeking and engaging with a supportive presence can pop me out of my anxious trance.

And there were bigger things. I had to also find faith to believe that my family was going to be fine. I had to believe I'd still have a job the following week, because there wasn't much good in thinking otherwise. And eventually, I had to believe that even if one of us did eventually come down with COVID, we'd survive that together, too.

My issues with anxiety have always made me a worst-case-scenario-type thinker, and that fed into all of this. The lack of faith comes from the belief that bad things are bound to happen. The hoarding and holing up fell in line with that, too.

I am working to someday get to a point of seeing the *best-case* scenario in all things and being more open to positive possibilities. This is a work in progress, but slogging through the pandemic at least got me to a point that allowed me to believe that even if things might not be amazing, they would at least be OK.

That basic belief was necessary for me to find the courage to eventually take baby steps back out into the world with my family. For me, the pandemic was a constant balancing act of caution and courage. How can we live our lives sensibly without being reckless or paranoid? I know this is something every individual and every parent grappled with during this time.

In the end, I think what I took away from the lockdown was that everyone needs to find their own zone of comfort, and then maybe push that boundary a little bit. Faith that today is good and tomorrow will be OK is an important foundation for that.

And one final note of advice: whether it be times of peace and prosperity or of pestilence and conflict, there is really no reason whatsoever to have more than two cans of cannellini beans in your pantry.

DO YOU REMEMBER?

The great toilet-paper shortage? In the opening months of the pandemic, as a society, we had to cope with numerous rapid changes and challenges to previous expectations of normalcy. Perhaps one of the most troubling was the sudden and shocking lack of toilet paper.

It's hard to conjure another product that is quite as taken for granted as toilet paper. We just assume it will always be there, so it came as a rather rude awakening when you suddenly couldn't find it in stores, and it became an incredibly valuable commodity.

The shortage was due in large part to consumer hoarding and supply-chain disruptions. Things eventually leveled out and you could find toilet paper and other paper products again, but many stores had per-customer limits for months.

It was yet another bizarre and unexpected turn in a time filled with bizarre and unexpected turns. And, for a time, we were all put in the position of asking, "Can you spare a square?"

CHAPTER 7

BEAUTIFUL BOY

It was day forty-three of my blog, April 27, 2020. In that day's post, titled "Baby's Got Back [Pain]," I made some lame jokes about my old, creaky back, referenced the Monkees, and wrote one of my many run-of-the-mill, just-another-day posts.

Except it wasn't just another day. It was the day that Erin and I received the diagnosis that Henry, following an assessment several weeks prior, had been identified as autistic.

I still remember writing that post, feeling torn and broken inside because of the news I had just received, not knowing how to talk about it. It felt so heavy, scary, and overwhelming at the time. I didn't know how to process it for myself, and I certainly didn't know how to write about it or talk to anyone else about it yet. Over the coming months, as we began dealing with the situation, I was wracked with fear, doubt, and stress—and I simply wrote around it in my blog. Even though I had set out to write honestly about our pandemic experience, I was being anything but forthright when it came to this part of lives.

I know what you're thinking. *Hold on. How could you possibly suppress those emotions and compartmentalize all of that without breaking face?* It isn't easy, but lest you forget, I am a German Catholic who grew up in a small town in Wisconsin. This sort of thing is second nature to me. If times are tough, you smile, push those feelings down deep, grind your teeth, and make a nice casserole.

The news was shocking, but not surprising. In our hearts, we long knew this was a possibility, even if my mind did everything possible to avoid accepting it.

Henry has always been very much his own person. That is one of the many things I love about him, but it also meant there were times, especially early on, where I felt like I didn't know how to help him. I still distinctly recall our first night together in the hospital after he had been born.

It was late at night. Erin was resting after giving birth, and I was spending time with my newborn son. He was a little agitated, and I could not soothe him. I used all the tricks that worked so well with Amelia, but nothing seemed to help.

His first year gave Erin and me PTSD. He would scream for hours, and he wouldn't sleep—there seemed to be one issue after another. We saw doctor after doctor and specialist after specialist. Henry always seemed to defy explanation. Doctors we worked with back then speculated that he had acid reflux, which could have explained the screaming and difficult nights, but even that was more a guess than anything.

After he reached a year old, he did seem to level out a little. He calmed down, the screaming and sleepless nights got better, but we still had our struggles. He crawled and walked quickly and was always extremely clever and mischievous. He was always impatient and on the move. His pediatrician theorized that he just didn't like being a baby and always wanted to be at the next step of development.

He was also speech delayed, and we had some concerns. His first word was "Wow," and for a very long time, that was his only word. While an excellent word to start with, we were hoping more were coming. We got him involved with a great early intervention program through the state of Colorado where he got speech therapy and occupational therapy until age three.

He made good progress, but when he reached three, we had to stop because the program only funded up to that age. Without further diagnosis, we couldn't get insurance support for more therapy, and at that time, we didn't suspect autism. We thought we were on a good path forward.

Henry likes to defy definition. He engages with people, he makes eye contact, he does a lot of things that go against a lot of the tired, old stereotypes of what society tells us autism looks like. Now, I understand how inaccurate those trendy "assessments" and online quizzes are, but we didn't know much better at the time. In preschool, Henry always played more alongside other kids than truly playing with other kids. "Parallel play," they call it. He wasn't making deep friendships. There were always little things that kept us wondering.

In fall of 2019, we talked to a few of our doctors who suggested maybe we should get him screened for autism, just in case. The thought was if he did get a diagnosis, at least we'd be able to get insurance to help cover therapy and support. The waiting list to get screened could be as far as a year out, so we figured we might as well get in line. In all that time, there were always ups and downs. Sometimes there would be stretches where he seemed just fine, and we thought he had turned a corner. But then he'd regress and have us wondering again.

In the end, I had myself pretty convinced we were just going through the motions with the autism assessment. I believed Henry was perfectly "normal" (whatever that means) and getting screened was just a formality. Looking back on it now, I can see the fear and denial I was experiencing—because I didn't know what autism was or what it would mean.

Then COVID came. Henry had been doing pretty well in pre-school, but we had to pull him out when the pandemic hit. We suddenly found ourselves able to move up in line for that autism assessment through Children's Hospital, because we were willing to do the assessment through this fancy new thing called "telehealth." Amazing, right? A doctor's appointment on your computer! Who knew?

We spent several hours talking online with a specialist, who listened intently and also observed Henry a little. As we went through the process, we answered tons of questions and relived so many moments in Henry's life. I remember having feelings pulling in both directions. On one side, the kinds of questions the specialist was asking made me think maybe he wasn't autistic. He could communicate well and had lots of skills that impressed the person conducting the assessment.

On the other hand, there were certain tells along the way that started to make it feel like there was something to this. His repetition and inability to move on from something he wants. The way he constantly pinched my hand and arm when he was trying to soothe himself, and other sensory cues we had picked up on.

We ended the nearly three-hour session and scheduled a follow-up a few weeks later, where we'd get the results of the assessment. At that point, I think we kind of left it to fate and I didn't know how to feel. With Henry, so often we'd meet with doctors and get him tested for this and that, convinced that we'd get an answer. But we had become accustomed to inconclusive results where Henry is concerned.

Then came April 27. We got on the call with Children's Hospital and learned that Henry is autistic. The definitions of what people refer to as the autism spectrum can be a little muddy, and it covers a wider range of issues than it has in the past. In a nutshell, what this identification told us was that he needed additional support in certain social, behavioral, and sensory areas.

It was a heavy dose of news to get right in the middle of a terrifying pandemic, and it was only the beginning. We had a lot to learn about ASD—what resources could be available, what insurance could and couldn't help with, and lots more. And we had to do all of this while the world was shut down, all of us cooped up together with uncertainty surrounding us. We were stressed out already, and I would be lying if I said this timing didn't make everything feel even scarier.

Our first instinct was to keep this news among ourselves and close family only. If I knew then what I know now, there are many parts of this journey I would have handled differently. In all the time leading up to learning this, we worried so much about the label and feared what it would mean for Henry. I worried about Henry having to deal with the stigma our society has built around autism. So initially, we decided to fight the fight quietly. And I made the choice to tiptoe around it in my writing rather than share what was becoming an increasingly large part of our lives.

I think one of the most important things we can do as parents— or as human beings—is look with clear eyes at moments when we were wrong, then admit we were wrong, and finally move forward and do better. This is an instance of a time when I was wrong. Full stop. I was wrong about how I saw things and how I approached the situation. It's important to share this because I sincerely hope it can help other parents avoid the same mistake.

It's not that I was necessarily *wrong* about initially keeping this information private. It took time for us to process it as a family, to learn about what it meant, and come up with a plan moving forward. It's natural to need space and time to find one's footing before talking with others about it.

What I was wrong about was my outward reasoning. I thought I was somehow protecting Henry by not telling anyone he was autistic. That wasn't protection; that was a product of my own fear and a lack of understanding.

In the time since we discovered Henry was autistic, I have learned so much about autism and neurodiversity, and now recognize it is not something to fear or shy away from. It is simply another dimension of the wonderful diversity of humanity. My son has talents, strengths, challenges, and foibles, just like any other child or adult does. He just needs a little extra support and understanding in some areas.

I've learned a great deal listening to adults with autism who are out in the world enjoying lives, jobs, and families—representing perspectives that are so important. What I've learned is that for decades, we've been taught to see that autism is this boogeyman lurking out there. It has long been presented as something to fear. And good heavens, if your child is identified as being autistic, that's the end of all your hopes and dreams.

That is terribly wrong. And as a society, we need to do a better job of seeing the truth. Yes, autism is a wide continuum, and there are certainly many families working with individuals whose situations are much more difficult and challenging than ours. But the important thing we learned is that help is out there, and this is just part of who our beautiful son is. It is not something to be feared. It is part of the grand tapestry of who Henry is and, frankly, something to be proud of.

Henry is incredibly smart and hardworking. He has a strong sense of self and possesses a will that I am honestly envious of. He remembers everything. He is hilarious and has an incredible sense of humor. What getting the assessment did for him and for our family was not the end of our hopes and dreams. It was the beginning. It allowed us to understand, learn, and do what we could do to support Henry becoming his best self. In those early days, I was so afraid of the label that I missed the true beauty and value of what we learned with his assessment: it unlocked a far deeper understanding of who Henry is and enabled us to see and support him more completely.

At the beginning, Children's Hospital walked us through the basics, but from there, we were pretty much on our own. We knew early intervention was important but had no idea what *kind* of intervention and how to find it. We were stepping into a vast, overflowing wilderness with no guide or compass. All we got were long, long faceless lists of providers for tons of different therapies and supports we didn't even understand. It was overwhelming and frightening, and we felt completely lost trying to figure it all out.

This is where Erin's strength and perspective were so vital to our trek through this unknown wilderness. While we were both shaken and initially struggling with the diagnosis, I credit my wife for shifting into action mode right away. Looking back, I can fully admit that I was in a deeper state of denial before the news, where I think Erin was more prepared for it. And she realized faster than I did that identifying the reality of the situation would only help us find a better way forward.

Erin is a tenacious and skilled researcher, and she dove into the endless lists of possible providers to find who could both help our son and best fit with our overall parenting and family philosophies. My role in those early days was mainly spending my time on hold with our insurance company and figuring out what support they would and would not cover. But Erin was the one who dedicated herself to finding the very best help for Henry.

From the beginning, we knew that what we were seeking was not to *change* Henry. We just wanted to help support who he is. Unfortunately, there is a lot of history in the autism-intervention world designed to just make autistic individuals "act normal," whatever that means. Our goals were to help Henry be confident and comfortable in his own skin, and Erin did an amazing job finding providers to facilitate that.

She did a great deal of reading and research to learn more about what the different kinds of available therapies were, what they did, and how they interacted with children on the spectrum. She made lots of calls and asked a lot of questions. We had long conversations about our shared parenting philosophy and made sure we were able to communicate that to potential providers, so we would know if they fit in with our goals as parents and as a family.

Erin had lots of phone conversations with potential providers and chiseled away at the list over time. The ones who made the final cut interviewed with all of us, either in person or via Zoom. For Henry, and for any kid, rapport means a lot, and his interactions with potential therapists told us a lot right out of the gate. Because Erin had done so much work qualifying the potential candidates ahead of time, making the final selections was that much easier.

In the end, we felt really good about the therapy team that we assembled, but getting there had been no easy task. As any family of an autistic child or a child with any disability would tell you, finding the right help feels needlessly challenging and ends up being a barrier for so many.

Most therapy centers were closed for COVID, but we were able to find some very good therapists who provided in-home support. This too was a strange and stressful moment of weighing risk and reward. We'd have to have people in our home during a time when we were avoiding human contact. But the therapists were masked, we took appropriate precautions, and we ultimately knew that getting Henry that help during this key time in his development was well worth the potential risk.

The question of whether masks were an obstacle for therapy and Henry's progress often comes up, and I know this has become a point of controversy for many people regarding schools and other education interactions. I will say, for our part—other than of course not being super fun to wear—I don't believe it caused any negative impact on Henry's progress. He was always good wearing masks or interacting with those who do. For us, the positives of being able to actually have in-home therapy safely during this time were more than worth it.

It was a lot of work at the beginning, and credit to Erin's tenacity, we got therapists who were great for and with Henry. Especially in the early days, the therapists took the time to play and have fun with Henry, which made all the difference for developing a rapport with him. Through games and imaginative play, the therapists made

Henry feel comfortable to be himself and created an environment where he felt good working with them.

One of the things Henry liked to do back then was act out scenes from movies and cartoons he loved. It was delightful to see these bright and dedicated therapists gleefully acting out scenes from *Peppa Pig* and *Space Jam* with our son, in between planned tasks and learning moments.

His therapy team was an ever-present part of our household for about a year. They really became part of our family, and we remain thankful for all their tireless efforts. Part of what made it work so well was the open lines of communication Erin and I kept up with the team. We took the time as parents to understand what they were doing and why so that we could help replicate and support those things as well.

We also spoke up when we thought something wasn't working. There was a time when we felt he was having to put in too many hours. And hard worker though he is, he is also a kid. We advocated for him, found a happy compromise solution with fewer hours, and he responded really well.

Learning about Henry's autism became an important subplot in our family's story during the COVID pandemic. At the time we received the news, it seemed like such a gut punch. *How can we possibly handle even* more *during already difficult times?*

But the fact is, the timing was exactly right. We learned more about who Henry is when many of the other distractions and pressures of the world were shut out, because we were basically on lockdown. It allowed us the time to focus on our son and pave a new road for our family.

And it changed our family as a whole and brought us even closer together. Amelia shined as the most amazing big sister anyone could ever ask for. She was not only encouraging and supportive of Henry, but she took an active part in helping during therapy sessions. She was there, playacting those scenes with Henry and his therapists, and participated in other learning activities for him. Henry adores his sister and I know her being there in those early days really helped him feel comfortable doing the challenging work.

This entire experience inspired Erin, who has now dedicated her professional life to helping families of children with disabilities, like ours. As she went through the confusing process of researching providers, discovering hidden state and federal support programs, and jumping through endless hoops, she asked aloud, "How are parents supposed to do this alone? It is so time consuming—so confusing and difficult. People deserve help."

So, in May of 2021, Erin launched a new business called Mountain Summit Coaching. She started out with the focus of helping families with children who have disabilities find providers and services. She has built an enormous network of providers, and through her navigation and parent coaching services, she helps families far and wide find their way to the kinds of successes we were able to achieve. As the business grew, she expanded into parent coaching for those with autistic children, and today she provides real holistic support to families who, like we once did, feel lost and confused.

And as for me, our work with Henry has given me so much perspective and a better understanding of my son and others who are neurodiverse. I help write content for Erin's business and have also written about disability parenting in a few local publications. I want to continue writing about this topic for a few reasons. One is to help parents like us find their way. It's a continuous process and there are many of us out there, so we should be supporting each other as much as possible.

The other reason is to foster a world where there is a greater acceptance and understanding of neurodiversity, so that neurodiverse and neurotypical people can meet in the middle—and individuals like my son won't have to be doing all the work in an ableist world.

It's idealistic of me, yes, but I still hope for a more equal and understanding society someday, somehow.

I am obviously biased, but honestly, Henry is just an amazing young fellow. He keeps growing by leaps and bounds. The little boy we worried about being speech delayed will now approach anyone he sees and chat them up. One of the things I delight in most since we started his therapy is that I can see how much more at ease he is with himself and the world. Before he was assessed and identified as autistic, he often felt off-balance and out of sorts. But now that we understand better how to support him, he is much more self-assured and comfortable in his own skin.

Henry graduated from several of his initial therapies but continues his occupational therapy and other supports at school, as well as at home. He has an individualized education program (IEP) at school. A music therapist still comes to our home, and Henry loves the sensory experience of playing his drums.

The pandemic years taught us a lot, and certainly COVID and its related impacts were one of the most obvious instructors. But Henry's journey was an important component of it for us. It also is an example of how the usual things in life didn't stop for the pandemic. This was our family's story, but other families faced their own unique odyssey. The other challenges and curveballs of life didn't stop just because there was a pandemic.

And all any of us parents could do was our best. When I look back on this time, I marvel at the behemoth level of work and research Erin did. I can also reflect on my own perception and see things to be proud of and things to improve on.

Parenting, like anything, is all swings and misses. None of us is always going to get it all right. Like in baseball, if you take swings, you are going to get strikes. If you don't swing, you never get a hit. We have to be ready to accept and learn from our successes and our failures.

After a few months of avoiding the topic in my daily blog, Erin and I had a conversation late that summer, and I finally concluded that I was, in fact, doing Henry a disservice by *not* talking about his being autistic. It was not something we felt ashamed of. It is not something he should *ever* be ashamed of. Autism isn't something anyone should feel negative feelings about. It is simply part of who our son is—one piece of a much larger whole.

At last, in late September of 2020, I wrote a post about Henry and a little bit about our path to that point. It was by far the most read and well-received post of the 450 I wrote in my blog. The love and support I received from it was overwhelming, and I also discovered that I knew several people who I was unaware had autistic children. It inspired me to write and talk more about it so we can hopefully move past the point where anyone thinks it remotely resembles a stigma.

Being autistic is something to be seen and understood for what it is: just another expression of the wonderful diversity that is humanity.

CHAPTER 8

THE HOWL

The world got pretty damn weird in those first few months of the COVID pandemic. It's easy to understand why, since everyone's lives were instantly turned upside down in a way none of us had experienced before. And we were all basically isolated, stuck inside, and going a little nutty.

There were lots of small ways that people everywhere tried to compensate for the isolation to find any way to feel a sense of unity. Where I was, just outside Denver, we had the 8:00 Howl.

I first noticed it about a month into the shutdown. By then, it had been going on in Denver for a while, and then took root out by us in the burbs. The concept was pretty simple: at 8 p.m. every night, people would go outside and howl as loud as they could. Like a bunch of damned werewolves.

At the time, I heard various stories as to why people were doing it. Kind of like an urban legend, everyone seemed to have a slightly different explanation. Some said it was a call to our animal nature, and indeed there could be something cathartic about that. Some said it was intended to support and honor medical first responders, which, um . . . OK. Not sure how that helps, but that's cool. And others just shrugged and thought *Hey, maybe it's just something weird to do.*

The 8:00 Howl was such a strange little sub-moment in the early-days-of-COVID-quarantine culture. When I went back much later to research it, I read some reporting about it in local newspapers and found its origins to still be pretty murky. Legend is that it was started by a Denver couple, Shelsea Ochoa and Brice Maiurro. Both community organizers, Ochoa is a performance artist and Maiurro is a poet and writer—so I'm imagining probably the kind of people who, in more normal times, would be found hanging around at Warhol's Factory or at Maude Lebowski's place.

Anyway, this wasn't long after we all saw the viral video of people singing from balconies in Italy, and we had all been through this unprecedented lockdown for long enough that the cravings for any kind of interaction were at lofty levels. I think the howling sort of played off of that.

According to one article I found about the Howl, like any good married couple, they each had a different origin story for the 8:00 Howl. Ochoa said she was inspired by people standing on a sand dune and howling at the sunset on a beach in Brazil. Maiurro, on the other hand, said it derived from gatherings he would have with a group of friends in Boulder, Colorado. They would stand in an alley during a full moon, recite poetry, and howl at the moon. I personally prefer the Brazil story. It's a lot more exotic, and a Brazilian beach is a way better setting than an alley in Boulder.

However it was inspired, the two of them pushed this idea of going out and howling at 8 p.m. every night by starting a Facebook group dedicated to the prospect, cleverly named "Go Outside and Howl at 8 p.m." Every night, a few more people in Denver would join in, and suddenly the page had a few hundred thousand followers, and the idea spread far and wide.

As I read about the backstory, I discovered that people did try to assign even more causes to the howl as it went along, whether it was autism awareness, a celebration of National Trans Day, or any other number of crusades. In the end, we all know that most good causes are best served by a bunch of people acting like a character from an old Tex Avery cartoon.

The 8:00 Howl went on loudly for at least a few weeks. Over time, it died down a little, but we had a nearby neighbor who was really into it. For a while, he seemed to be the one howl source in our neighborhood. I remember one night when Amelia and Henry stood up on their little plastic backyard fort and joined in, howling as loudly as they could. That was the first time I thought the Howl was kind of cute.

Our dog, Asta, found it vexing. She became very protective of our house during the pandemic. Anyone who dared walk near the house—or sneeze within a block of it—was going to get barked at. I would have thought, given her hair-trigger barking, that she would go bananas with all this primal racket and be convinced that our home was under siege by feral wolves or something.

But at 8 p.m. every night, she would just look out and stare. She didn't bark or freak out. Just looked out, puzzled. Is it possible that, like me, she just found it to be kind of dumb? Dogs are very clever, after all.

Back then, I rolled my eyes at the Howl every single night. But in retrospect, I have to say, I have some respect for the idea behind it. It was this attempt for everyone to vocalize and remind each other that we're still here. There was something ancient and elemental about it. It's possible that I took part once or twice.

And on the other side, I think there was also something a little chilling about it. We were deep in early-stage fear, and I couldn't help but wonder if it signified something more frightening. Like a breakdown in our well-ordered civilization and a reversion to a natural-state anarchy waiting at the gates.

I am not one who takes civilization for granted. We've all lived in it our whole lives. And sure, it's easy to assume that it only grows, goes forward, and gets better. History, however, shows that isn't always true.

Disaster, climate changes, and famine have derailed plenty of civilizations before, and we are not immune. Literally. We were faced with a fast-spreading disease and were defenseless. Nature still can kick us around quite effectively.

Things can break down when enough people get sick, scared, or desperate. It turned out, in our case, it wasn't so much an end of civilization as it was an end of polite decorum. We suddenly had people starting dumb fights over mask wearing and encroaching on our six feet of personal space. I think the pandemic tore at the already-frayed edges of our society. The forces of division—whether political, social, racial, cultural—were already pulling things apart, and the pandemic only served to accelerate all those forces.

Maybe in the end, the Howl was a good idea to try to pay tribute to our inner connection to the wild, while still living in a society that allows us to live together and supports things like performance art and poetry.

Or maybe it was just something to do at 8:00 every night before you settled in to start binging another Netflix series. Either way.

DO YOU REMEMBER?

Tiger King? That was such a big thing for a while, and seemingly the only thing that was exposed to more people than COVID itself.

During a strange and stressful time where many people were looking for ways to stave off madness driven by isolation and boredom, this cultural phenomenon became part of a trend of people binge watching shows and pseudo-documentaries about very, very strange people.

CHAPTER 9

RITUAL DE LO HABITUAL

We live in a self-improvement culture, and I'm as much a consumer of that as anyone. It probably has roots in my long-standing feelings of insecurity and inadequacy. It's that voice inside my head that is always saying *Yeah, OK. But is that the best you can do?*

I have named that voice Carl. I'm not going to lie, he is kind of an asshole. If he invites you to dinner, find an excuse not to go.

For many years I have sought out ways to improve myself and grow as a person. And the more I do it, the more it feels like a healthy pursuit of constantly attempting to learn new things and move forward, rather than just trying to satisfy the insatiable voice of Carl.

Long before COVID, I had been reading books and listening to podcasts to sharpen myself professionally, to center myself spiritually, and to find my lane as a writer. In fact, about a month before COVID hit, I invested in screenwriting software because that was something I wanted to dabble in again after taking a couple decades off.

When COVID burst onto the scene and all of us were in some version of quarantine, there was suddenly this major cultural wave of talk and even pressure to use this time to better ourselves. In my recollection of those first few months, a lot of the buzz on social media was either about which streaming shows to binge watch or what new skills and habits we should be building.

There was *Tiger King* and the baking craze, for example. I never bought into either of those. But I was drawn to the idea of healthy habits. I have plenty of bad habits—procrastination, disorganization, midnight candy snacks, hanging out with Carl—but what if I were to have some *good* habits?

Without really realizing it, I started working on a significant healthy habit when I had the idea to write a blog, on literally Day One of the lockdown. I had tried and failed to write blogs a bunch of times over the years and always lost steam or got bored. And this one started as a real off-the-cuff idea.

The first day with the kids off from "extended spring break," things got pretty chaotic pretty quickly, and I saw tons of parents posting notes of angst or quarantine activity suggestions for kids. So, I had the idea of starting a little Facebook group for my parent friends, cleverly named "P's and Q: Parenting, Productivity, and Quarantine."

A bunch of people accepted the invitation and began posting. That day, I thought I'd write a little post about our experience so there'd be some content on the page. And without knowing it, I set sail on a voyage for the next 450 days that would ultimately end with me penning this book.

After writing one post, I decided to do it the next day, and then the next day. At that point, I didn't figure this whole quarantine thing would last more than a couple weeks, so I thought *What the hell, I'll just keep writing these every day.*

People would read my posts, which were generally about whatever we had done that day, some wacky story about the kids, or my thoughts on that particular moment in the pandemic. Readers would like or make a comment here or there out of solidarity. It wasn't like I had an enormous following or anything; it was friends and family. But what it *did* do is supply me with one of the most important elements in any habit-building exercise: accountability.

A few weeks went on, then a few months, and I was still writing every day. Some posts were more substantive and thought out while others were just messy freewriting at the end of the day. No kidding, there were many posts that I wrote with one hand because my left arm was wrapped around Henry as I performed the forty-five-minute exercise of soothing him and getting him to bed.

People would sometimes say, "I'm surprised how many typos and formatting errors are in your posts! You used to be an editor, right?"

All true. And looking back on some of those posts, many are mangled messes. But polished prose was honestly not the point. In fact, in many ways, those hackneyed posts kind of *were* the point.

Because what I was doing was building a habit. At first kind of by accident, later by design, I was pushing myself into building a writing habit. And like many writers, procrastination was part of my problem, based on the inner editor voice (Thanks, Carl) saying *If something isn't perfect, you shouldn't write it.*

This doesn't apply only to writing. How many of us have thought about starting something and never doing it because we are afraid of not getting it right? I had to get over that hump and not worry about writing something perfect. I just needed to get into the habit of writing something every day; maybe not something perfect, glorious, or even spellbinding, but *something*. By the time I reached a month of consecutive posts, I was having days that were **hard**, where I'd come within a hair's breadth of breaking the streak and not writing anything.

Research says that habits are constructed on three essential pillars: cue, routine, and reward.

The cue is the thing that triggers the behavior. In my case with the blog, it would probably best be described as time. I would generally write about the previous day, usually at or after the kids' bedtime.

The routine was the actual act of writing itself. And here's where I had to shed a lot of the concerns about the quality of what I was writing, accepting that there would be days that resulted in good content and other days would be lackluster. I needed to convince myself that was OK, because the goal was the routine.

And then there is the reward, which in my case was kind of a mix of a positive and negative reinforcement mechanism. I would absolutely feel reward in a blog post getting a few likes or comments; that was the positive side. But there was also the other side of it, which motivated me to write for fear that people would notice if I *didn't* keep to the routine. That was the accountability piece.

This is not to say anyone would have called me out or castigated me if I missed a day. But just the idea of the public nature of the blog helped me. It mixed in with my own sense of will to keep this thing going.

While writing the blog, I often described it as a dare I made with myself to keep writing. It turned into a game of chicken—me versus Carl—and the longer it went on, the more I didn't want to give in and yield.

It was hard. There were days it was *very* hard. And there were days I was so exhausted or stressed that each finger stroke felt like agony. But I kept pushing through it because I wanted to get to a place where daily writing felt natural and not forced.

In retrospect, I don't know if that level of insane dedication was required to form the habit, but what I can report is that for me, it did work. The more time that passed, the more comfortable I became in my own skin as a writer. That inner editor voice faded dramatically, and it made a difference in the writing I do for myself, and also the writing I do professionally.

While this was the most dramatic example of habit-building I undertook during the pandemic, I also applied some of the same principles to other positive habits for my health and overall mental and spiritual well-being. Creating some good routines helped me get back to regular daily exercising and healthier eating. I also found moments in the day for things like journaling and self-care that are important for body and soul.

Like many parents, I often feel like there just aren't enough hours in the day. I'm always scrambling to get things done, and even then, I am still behind. I spent a lot of time fretting about how is it possible to build in time for things like exercise, writing, or other pursuits when I already can't find enough time to do what I need to do?

I found that the answer is starting very small and being OK with allocating a mere ten minutes for writing or fifteen minutes for running. Something is better than nothing. Once you start creating those habit loops, it's amazing how you can suddenly turn around and find that it becomes second nature.

I still nab candy late at night sometimes. And I still probably let Carl drone on a little too much, but at least I've got some good habits in the rotation now, too.

EXCERPT FROM JIM'S ABANDONED BOOK OF COVID KNOCK-KNOCK JOKES

Knock knock!
Who's there?
Hydroxychloroquine.
Hydroxychloroquine who?
Hydroxychloro-can you believe people were taking horse paste to stop COVID?

CHAPTER 10

THE MASTER'S WHEEL

"This is called a training circle, a master's wheel. This circle will be your world, your whole life. Until I tell you otherwise, there is nothing outside of it . . . As your skill . . . improves, you will progress to a smaller circle. With each new circle, your world contracts, bringing you that much closer to your [goal]."   —Don Diego de la Vega, *The Mask of Zorro*

One afternoon, Amelia and Henry were in the backyard having a play sword fight with a cardboard tube and a plastic bat. They were laughing and running around, and it made me smile, bringing back memories of my own childhood doing the exact same thing with my siblings and cousins.

At this particular time, there were a few squares and circles in our small backyard, marked off with a kind of vinyl tape over the grass. This was for a little canine agility course Erin had put together for Asta. For those of you not familiar with the sport, agility is an activity where dogs basically go through cool little obstacle courses. There are tunnels, jumps, weaves, and all kinds of things. It's sort of like *American Gladiator* or *The Floor is Lava*, but for dogs.

For humans and canines alike, the early pandemic was a time where we all grabbed hold of whatever diversions or activities could keep us sane for the indeterminate period we'd be stuck in our homes. The agility course was a simple little thing that was entertaining for Asta, while also providing a fun little spectator sport for us humans.

Seeing the kids in their fencing stances among these taped-off shapes made me think of one of my favorite adventure movies from the 1990s, *The Mask of Zorro*. In the movie, the aging, retired Zorro (played by Anthony Hopkins) trains a young ex-bandit (played by Antonio Banderas) to take his place.

> ***RANDOM TANGENT:*** *At this very moment writing this, it occurred to me that both of those actors could, in theory, be called "Tony" on the set. But my hunch is no one ever calls either one of them "Tony." How did I never notice that?*

I digress.

Specifically, my backyard reminded me of the first scene in the training montage, where the elder Zorro describes what he calls "The Master's Wheel." Thinking about that scene made me view the experience of pandemic parenting through an entirely new lens.

This experience—being confined to our homes for an extended period of time— for parents and people everywhere, was our own Master's Wheel. Our own individualized training circle.

In de la Vega's description of it, the Master's Wheel exists to shut out the distractions of the outer world and create a limited space for focus and concentration on self-development. Outside of it, there is nothing. It narrows the focus inward.

And as you master the outer circle, you move inward to smaller, more precise circles until mastering the final circle—your inner self. Conquering this feat, you would be the true master of yourself and theoretically prepared to deal with whatever adversaries await in the outer world.

For me (and I suspect many people), the pandemic had many of the qualities of this Master's Wheel exercise. By necessity, COVID closed out many of the focus-diluting things of everyday life and put me in a position of being able to work inward toward those progressively smaller circles.

This played out in all facets of my life. On a professional level, it gave me the opportunity to develop, focus, and improve what I do. When COVID hit, I had been running a small regional trade association for a little less than a year. It was going well, but I hadn't really found my own footing just yet. I was basically doing a lot of what my predecessor did, stepping nervously into some new areas, often a little light on confidence.

The pandemic turned everything, including my job, upside down. This was terrifying at first. A lot of my job had been delivering education in the offices of architects and engineers. When nobody could get together or gather indoors anymore, that was all thrown out the window.

What started out frightening turned into an opportunity for me and the organization. Using the Master's Wheel as a template, I took that time to shrink my world to a smaller circle and focus on the development of my professional self and the job itself. Instead of doing what others had done, I took this opportunity to find new ways to accomplish the goals of my position and mold the role to my strengths. The constricted circle allowed me to get creative and find new ways to get our organization's message out, even in challenging times.

I started taking chances, because what else could I do? Since office interactions were shut down, I began developing more online content and repositioning our organization to effectively deliver education presentations virtually. I started forming relationships with local and regional organizations that helped connect me to larger groups. By the end of 2020, I had considerably more course attendees and contact points than I had pre-pandemic.

That's not to say everything worked, because some didn't. I went a little Zoom crazy in the early days and tried hosting some virtual membership meetings and even tried planning an online conference.

The conference never got off the ground, and attempted virtual meeting was a straight-up flop. What I learned is that the value of those membership meetings isn't whatever reports or presentations I come up with, the value is in the networking that takes in and around the meeting. So in the future, as restrictions eased a little, I found ways to plan reasonably safe outdoor activities for people to get together in person.

The lesson in all of it was that I needed to stop being afraid of trying and start throwing new ideas against the wall. By doing that, not only did I improve the effectiveness of our organization, I also grew as a person. And for maybe the first time in my professional life, I made the job match *me* more than making me match the job.

By the time COVID restrictions somewhat eased, it turned out I had progressed pretty far toward that final, inner circle. I felt more confident in myself and my job, was doing it better, and now had access to the tools that were available to me before the pandemic, in addition to the new strategies I'd developed during the pandemic.

It was, of course, challenging to work at home with kids running around at all times. But when the kids finally went back to school, the skill of balancing everything during the pandemic sharpened my focus and time management, making me more effective.

The same was true in my role as a parent. The limitations of quarantine gave me the ability to shut out much of the anxious noise that typically distracted me and focus on my family and my place in it. I didn't have to travel for a long time and could truly be present. Writing my daily blog was a big piece of my training in my personal and parental Master's Wheel. Taking the time to chronicle each day and the special moments, big and small, really showed me the value of each day and the importance of being there.

I built so many special memories with my children during lockdown. Even with the horror and ugliness of that time, I will always treasure those small moments. Things like inventing holidays and playing dress up and making up new games and imaginary worlds to explore were all part of our coping mechanism and brought lots of smiles and laughs even on tough days. The time in the training circle reminded me of the value of play and showed me how joining your kids in their imaginary worlds deepens your relationships with them out here in the real world.

Putting the safety and health of our families above all was the North Star for many of us raising pandemic-era kids. We all might have had different ideas about exactly what that means or meant, but one thing I learned was that it is bad form to judge anyone else for how they approach parenting—during the 2020 lockdown or any time. Everyone had different comfort levels, and all anyone could do was their best.

In our case, we were super cautious about being out in the world. But as time went on, we dipped our toes in and tried to venture out as safely as possible, thinking that some kind of mental balance was important. I know some families who were much more cautious than we were, some with immunocompromised family members who were at higher risk. Other families I know were completely out in the world, calculating that the risks were worth it.

I have always felt that parenting is like jazz improv—we do our best and make it up as we go. I am extremely dubious of anyone claiming superior knowledge of exactly how things are done as a parent. But parents always feel the pressure of being judged and not doing something "correctly."

One of things the pandemic helped me understand was that it doesn't much matter what anyone else thinks. We each, as people and as parents, need to understand what our own guiding principles and boundaries are. We follow those, acknowledging that not everyone is going to always agree. We may not all be playing in the same key, but we are all playing the same instrument.

It's not like pre-pandemic I was making decisions heavily influenced by others and their perception. But others' approval bothered me more in those days. After time in the Master's Wheel, one realizes the importance of staying true to oneself on one's journey. For my family, the guiding principle was always our health, safety, and wellness—the foundation of our decisions.

The pandemic era also taught me how to truly see and understand my kids. Not to say I didn't know them before. But we had such a limited scope on *one* thing (i.e., COVID) that removed usual distractions and allowed for a deeper understanding. I don't know if it was by coincidence or universal design, but getting Henry's autism diagnosis early in the pandemic was a blessing. The world being closed down allowed us to really be with him and work with him during that vital time of transition for him.

With help from a great team of therapists, Henry gained a new confidence and skills. Before, he always felt kind of volcanic and filled with angst. He would explode if we couldn't load the show he wanted to watch fast enough, or if we didn't have the snack he wanted. We struggled to understand each other. I know the difficulty communicating and getting his point across gave him endless frustration and put a short fuse on his temper.

From his support team, Henry learned many coping and communication skills, and we learned how to help support him and create the kind of dialogue and understanding we never had before. We worked hard on learning how to better understand his cues and helping him express his thoughts and feelings. After just a few months, we found that he had developed the emotional self-awareness to know when he is feeling overwhelmed and needs to take a break.

Before he would just rise over the threshold and explode. But as we worked together, he learned to actually ask for help and support when he needs it. He was able to advocate for himself and be open about his feelings and needs. At age five! I know plenty of people at age *forty*-five who aren't so great with that.

When restrictions eased and Henry was able to go to in-person kindergarten, the techniques we worked on together made all the difference. I know that our time in the Master's Wheel, all the work he had put in during the previous year, set him up for success in school and life in general. The journey, of course, goes on and on, but I think we are thankful for the positive course he has been set on.

For Amelia, I saw how a very social little girl, who always loved being around her friends at school, could progress through her own Master's Wheel. She eagerly took on the challenge of online schooling and learned that not all-important connections are in person. She worked hard and went out of her way to engage other kids struggling to connect in the surreal world of virtual school. She worked hard on her academics and did her very best to connect with peers and teachers, even while at a distance during that difficult time.

This by no means is to say it was easy for her; it wasn't. For many kids, it was even tougher. It was particularly rough during the first few weeks while she wrapped up first grade, when there wasn't much of a framework set up. She had to do a lot of independent work, and it just felt like being saddled with tons of homework all the time.

When she started virtual second grade in the fall, things were better. And Amelia, always the optimist and positive force, immediately embraced her new online teacher and classmates. She worked hard and would always participate in any group activities online, even the optional ones. The teacher would set up discussions, and sometimes Amelia was the only one there. She craved that social interaction, and I worried how she would do being cut off during the pandemic.

But with the remarkable adaptability of a younger generation, Amelia seemed to do very well with virtual interaction as a temporary replacement. She obviously preferred seeing people in person, but she talked glowingly of her class and her groups in virtual school the same way she did in person.

When restrictions eased and Amelia went back to in-person school, she seemed to embody all the best of her pre-pandemic and pandemic skills and strengths combined. She went right back to being a social magnet and made tons of new friends at a new school. Her newfound confidence and flexibility made it easier for her transition and to succeed in a new school, where she continues to be a leader, advocating for herself and her friends.

For Erin, the journey of the pandemic Master's Wheel was also sometimes difficult, yet inspiring and transformative. At the beginning of COVID, she was launching her health coaching business. Erin had struggled with many postpartum health issues, and she was dedicated to helping other women deal with issues that society and many doctors just plain ignore. She worked so hard for months taking a certification course and then building the foundation to launch a business.

But it all came to a screeching halt, as the world did, when COVID came into the picture. There was no more going out to network or doing all the things she needed to do to promote her service and bring in clients. Everyone was withdrawing, and the timing didn't end up being right for that business at that moment.

Like the rest of us, she turned her focus inward and helped the kids through online school. Then, following Henry's being identified as autistic in April, she pivoted her attention full-time to finding the best support and services for him—which I've mentioned was extremely challenging and time-consuming—and she discovered she was very good at it.

As any parent of a child with a disability can tell you, the process following the diagnosis is so overwhelming, confusing, and scary. There's no roadmap to getting help or outlining what kind of help is even needed. Fortunately for Henry and our whole family, Erin is an ace at research and getting things done. She dove mightily into learning more about the available therapists and providers.

This inspired her to launch a new business in 2021. The immense challenge Erin and our family struggled through to get help for Henry made her realize how hard it is for families everywhere. So, Erin's time in the Master's Wheel revealed a new passion and skill set. In spring of 2021, she launched a new business dedicated to helping families like ours navigate these difficult waters, find the help they need for their children, and get the support they deserve.

I can simultaneously hold to the truth that, for me, I came through the pandemic with limps and scars, but also as a more fully-fledged person than I was when it started. It was hard. I had moments of severe anxiety and fear and had to walk through that, really facing down who I am and where I want to go. I felt overwhelmed and exhausted, but also discovered that I could build good and productive habits without burning myself out. The pandemic taught me so much and gave me the opportunity to grow. I don't think I would have had the courage to write this book without my time in the Master's Wheel. I wouldn't be the person, the parent, or the professional I am today without it.

If you look, I'm sure you'll find examples of evidence or growth that wouldn't necessarily have happened on a non-COVID timeline. Maybe it's just a few new and healthy habits, or maybe it's a deeper understanding of yourself or your family. Even seemingly small steps forward can prove to be enormous. For me, there were many. Being present with my wife and kids, cooking and eating with health and purpose in mind, moving my body for physical activity each day. Every little thing matters.

COVID changed the world and every individual in it. It's up to us what to make of that change. Bad things and bad times happen. It is an absolute and something we ultimately have very little control over. What we *can* control is that inner circle—who we are and what we make of things.

Scars and all, I endeavor to make something as positive as possible out of those years and keep stepping forward. The training continues and always will. We keep moving to the next circle, and as de la Vega said, "With each new circle, your world contracts, bringing you that much closer to your [goal]."

DO YOU REMEMBER?

Washing down groceries? In late March of 2020, a Michigan doctor posted a video that went viral, showing people how to disinfect groceries and carryout that came in the house.

Of course, we later learned that COVID-19 spreads almost exclusively through the air. But at the time, so little was known about this scary virus that the whole idea of treating the things you buy at the store like a hazmat situation seemed perfectly reasonable.

People all across the nation set up separate stations and added this exhausting procedure to their already stressful grocery shopping routines. For most, the procedure generally fizzled out after a few months, either because new data showed surface transmission wasn't anything to be all that worried about, or because people just got really, really, really sick of doing it and would rather take their chances with COVID.

CHAPTER 11

THE LONG AND DISTANT GOODBYE

Life slams us with ups and downs and mixed emotions during even the best of times. Those ups and downs seemed enhanced on steroids during a time when a pandemic raged, people had been inside for months, lives and livelihoods were in danger, and basic concepts of reality seemed to be defined by opinion, beliefs, and who was yelling the loudest.

In May of 2020, a good indicator of how far down the rabbit hole we were was the fact that the Air Force released honest-to-god footage of UFOs, and it barely made the news. I suppose at that point, an alien invasion might have been a nice change of pace. Particularly if they were cool and funny aliens, like from planet Ork. Shazbot!

Those were hard days. Battle lines were being drawn in states and communities about the merits of "opening up" or continuing with shutdowns and public health precautions. Grown-ups were facing so many challenges on so many fronts, but I thought often about how this affected our kids. I know kids are adaptable in many ways, but what a strange thing this was to have to adapt to. Life as they knew it has been turned upside-down.

For the most part, our kids were amazingly resilient through it all. Ours played and laughed and smiled, but you could also see the stress come out in subtle ways. Amelia is an extremely social child and missed her friends and outside family quite a bit. Near the beginning of the shutdown, she would love getting on FaceTime with people. But after a few months, when offered, she would often politely decline. She would still frequently talk about the people she missed but tended to lean toward putting off calls and focusing on what was there on that day. I get that. Frankly, I felt a little inward retreat in those days, too.

School was another point of difficulty. That abrupt shift to online learning spring of 2020 was a mess, certainly in our district and I'm sure nationwide, as well. There was just no playbook or infrastructure for it. By Fall of 2020, our district had a pretty good system in place, and I salute all educators who battled through those days because it was a nearly impossible ask. And I think they did really well under extraordinarily difficult circumstances.

Amelia was really struggling at the end of her 2020 school year and getting tired of all the homework. Erin and I helped her power through as best we could, always telling her the end of the school year was in sight. But as it was for so many kids, the transition was difficult. There was so little structure in those early days. Basically, the class would meet over Zoom for maybe a half an hour in the morning and then the kids would have to log in to a handful of different learning platforms to complete activities and schoolwork.

There are plenty of adults in the world who struggle doing self-directed work—expecting it of a first-grader was a pretty big ask. Even a kid as responsible as Amelia was having trouble pushing through it all. I think it was being in this strange situation where she was home in what felt like a non-school day, but then was expected to do a bunch of homework. Even though it was fewer hours and less work than traditional school, it still felt like an extra drag to her, and I couldn't blame her.

Add to that the fact that the poor girl was trying to work through all the emotions of the scary world of 2020, and it was a recipe for a totally understandable rough slog. But even with some occasional grumbling and arguing, Amelia was a real trouper and made it through those closing weeks of the semester with aplomb. She got very excited for her last day of school, and even got all her homework for that week done early. But she also sweetly talked about how much she missed her teacher and wished she could see her again.

Always the kind of child who forms close bonds with her teachers, Amelia had a very tight connection to her first-grade teacher. She was an important person in Amelia's life, and it was hard having that yanked away so suddenly, only being able to connect through a screen.

On one of the last days of that semester, I overheard Amelia in her morning Zoom class. At the end, the teacher offered to stick around a little longer if any of the kids wanted to stay and chat. Amelia immediately raised her hand. It turned out, she was the only one. She had a nice, one-on-one conversation with her teacher. They talked about things they liked to watch, things they wanted to do in the summertime—regular stuff.

Amelia's first-grade teacher was incredible. She was so sweet and wonderful and was such a great presence in our daughter's life. She fostered a real enthusiasm and love of learning in Amelia. We were going to miss her almost as much as Amelia, and I was glad the two of them could have that one-on-one moment together.

That afternoon was the designated pickup at school. Parents could drive through and pick up the belongings that the students left behind before they went on unexpected "extended spring break" back in March. Erin took Amelia in the drive-through line to pick up her things.

Upon returning, Amelia was happy to see all her stuff—some books she had been working on, cool art projects, supplies, and other odds and ends. Most notable, though, was a little bag of candy and a kind note from Amelia's teacher, telling her what a great student she was and how proud she was of her.

As Amelia read it, I think Erin and I got more emotional than she did. Amelia was super happy about the candy and bounced away, happy.

Then a little while later, I saw Amelia sitting by herself, staring at that letter from her teacher. She sat quietly with it for quite a while.

She didn't have to say anything, but I knew how much that letter meant to her. And how hard this all was for her. She was excited to be done with school, but sad to move on. Life is like that. It doesn't matter how old you are. These kinds of transitions are bittersweet, more so when you can't get a hug from that teacher who meant so much to you.

A few days later, the teachers from the school did a little driving parade around our neighborhood so at least the kids could wave and say goodbye. It was fun, but also sad and bittersweet. Amelia was so excited to see her teacher drive by. We were thankful that after the parade, her teacher even took the time to stop by our house and sneak a quick hug outside.

In the depths of my early-pandemic anxiety and paranoia, I remember a fleeting feeling of concern stir in my brain as they embraced, but even then, I immediately dropped it. It helped that Erin was there to help me see there were bigger, more fragile emotions at play, and she edged me off my viral anxiety. I understood even then that the emotional connection happening was so much more important. It became difficult to know what was right and what was wrong. But in the end, we are humans with needs that go beyond CDC guidelines. It can be a tricky tightrope to walk, for sure, but we all did our best.

This pandemic affected every one of us, young and old. And let me be clear, I was glad that the schools were closed at that particular time. It was hard for so many reasons, but there was so much we didn't or couldn't know in those first few months. Based on the knowledge we had then, I believe it was the right thing to protect the health of our kids and our communities.

I recognize, however, that there were costs. Not being in school impacted the kids, of course. There is much work still to be done to make many kids whole after the pandemic years. There was no ideal option, but when push comes to shove, I will always incline toward caution related to basic health and life safety.

Those were difficult times that often seemed to present us with no-win scenarios. We had to do our best to adapt and adjust. Change can be hard. It had its costs, but there are upsides, too. We came out better on the other side. Humans are creatures of habit, and this can be hard to remember sometimes, but adaptability is one of our species' greatest assets. I witnessed it and still see it in my little ones every day.

EXCERPT FROM JIM'S ABANDONED BOOK OF COVID KNOCK-KNOCK JOKES

Knock knock!
Who's there?
Disinfectant.
Disinfectant who?
Disinfect-ain't it hard to find disinfectant during COVID-19?

CHAPTER 12

HYPOCHONDRIAC BLUES

There's really no good time to be a hypochondriac. It's a drag, and it's not fun to be that person who thinks that every oddball bump or pain that pops up is probably cancer. It is a constant cause of stress and can also lead to lots of doctor's appointments where you shell out a copay just to be told by a licensed medical professional that you don't have Ebola or rickets.

I say this as someone who has struggled with these kinds of issues in my long, rich history of anxiety. While never officially diagnosed as a hypochondriac, I absolutely have had that tendency of worrying and fretting about every absurd possibility of disease and death. And is there anything more hypochondriac than self-diagnosing as a hypochondriac without real evidence or professional assessment?

Not that there isn't plenty of evidence in my corner for this label. Back around 2005, I instituted an official ban on myself for ever visiting WebMD. I couldn't go on that website without leaving convinced I had some obscure pox that could only be treated by Dr. House.

While I've come a long way with my mental health since those days and have tamed some of my more severe hypochondriac impulses, it still is certainly something I have to contend with. It had been reasonably under control . . . until COVID-19 came into the picture.

Particularly in those early days, when so little was known about coronavirus, it was terrifying to all of us. But there is something particularly devious about it, to those of us who have this germaphobe-doomsday streak. Now we had to worry about a virus whose symptoms were so broad they basically mimicked all the usual stuff that you might pick up just walking around.

I have lots of seasonal allergies and frequently wake up with a dry, itchy, or sore throat. During COVID, every time I felt that, I snapped awake thinking *COVID!!!! It's doom! Ready the ventilator and bring my favorite blankie to the death bed!*

Stuffiness? Check. I always have that. Loss of smell? You bet. I've had an awful sense of smell since I was a kid, so really it's possible I've had COVID since the late '70s.

All throughout the pandemic, I'd have moments of terror thinking that a little nasal drip was going to turn out to be COVID. To drill down to my deepest feelings about my hypochondria, my primary concern was less about myself actually getting COVID than it was about being the disease vector that spreads it to my wife and children.

For reasons that escape me, particularly given everything I've just mentioned, I actually have a pretty sturdy immune system. I'm not exactly sure why. Yes, I try to stay reasonably healthy, but not nearly to the extent of my wife, who once studied to be a health coach and is one of the most well-informed people I know when it comes to nutrition and well-being.

Yet, very often, colds and flus will rampage through the house and take everyone down except me. Amelia also seems to have a resistant immune system, but Erin and Henry seem to pick up whatever is coming through and struggle to fight it off.

That was where a lot of my anxiety was focused. Particularly before we were all vaccinated, I was worried about any possibility of passing COVID on to Erin, Henry, or Amelia. So, I took every precaution I could and spent plenty of pointless energy fretting over every sniffle.

Sure, my heart may have been in the right place, but it is straight-out embarrassing. I'd have days where I felt a little sore throat or something and worry incessantly about it, but unsure whether to bring it up to my wife or not. She is wonderful and knows my tendencies in this area all too well, but even in that context, I felt like a big worrywart doofus.

When home tests were available, sometimes I took them to make sure. Other times, I just waited a few hours or a day, and sure enough, I felt fine soon.

It took on another dimension on the rare occasions that I would have to travel for work or give a presentation somewhere in person. In the Before Times, I traveled frequently and brought home any number of colds or ailments from airplanes and airports. I'll admit, I'm giving serious thought to just always wearing masks from now on for air travel because, let's face it, whether it's COVID or anything else, air travel is a stew of viruses and bacteria.

I remember being particularly concerned about a work trip I had to take to Texas in early December of 2021. It occurred right at the time that Omicron was starting to break into the news cycle, and I was traveling to a state not super well-known for COVID precautions. I was with a small group who I knew to be vaccinated, but I was still plenty nervous.

Not only was I worried about bringing COVID home, but I was also worried about messing up the trip to Disneyland we were planning for the week after Christmas. I remember sitting in meetings, running numbers through my head thinking *OK, if I get infected today and become symptomatic in four days, this is the timeline of potential spread and infection . . .*

It is ninety-five kinds of sad that I sat there looking at the calendar wondering *If the worst happens and I got COVID, will it run its course soon enough for us to go to Disneyland?*

I'm sure after getting home, I had at least a day or two where I wondered if a little throat congestion was COVID. Thankfully, it wasn't; our whole Disneyland trip worked out. But it goes to show how much time and energy an anxious mind will spend spinning possible scenarios that may very well never come to pass.

Did our family ever get hit by the COVID bug? As of the writing of this, I'll be honest, I'm not super sure. In April of 2022, everyone except me got taken down by a really nasty something that may well have been COVID, though the at-home tests came back negative. It's still entirely possible it did make its way through the house, though thankfully we were all vaccinated, and whatever it was left us intact. Most studies indicate we've all probably had the virus in some form or fashion by now, and I doubt our family is any exception. At least so far, we are all fortunate to be doing OK.

It is a difficult time to be a hypochondriac, but this has also taught me to work even harder at avoiding the mental trap of creating problems that may or may not be real. I tried to pull back and put myself in the default position of assuming good news instead of bad, therefore assuming that a throat tickle is just a throat tickle, not COVID. Or that a random ache in my back is a muscle strain and not some new and obscure form of cancer.

It's a work in progress, to be sure, but COVID has certainly forced me to up my game in this area. And in case you're wondering, yes, I still stay way the hell away from WebMD.

DO YOU REMEMBER?

The Bakersfield doctors? By April of 2020, just about a month into the lockdown, society was starting to fray, and disagreements over the severity—or even existence—of COVID pulled people into different camps. This was accomplished largely through what has become the traditional language of our times: viral online videos.

Two urgent-care doctors from Bakersfield, California, shared a video presenting some of their own, back-of-the-napkin, anecdotal evidence that COVID wasn't any worse than the flu, and people should stop worrying about it and feel comfortable coming back to their urgent care. They wore scrubs in the video, to appear as medical as possible.

The video inspired lots of people to call for the removal of closures and mandates, and also inspired strong rebukes from infectious disease specialists and others with actual expertise and real-time data on this issue. The American College of Emergency Physicians and the American Academy of Emergency Medicine declared they "emphatically condemn the recent opinions" of the doctors.

It was among the first of what would be many questionable stances by medical and non-medical professionals whose expertise was not in the area of infectious disease. The video was, however, perhaps the most notable news out of Bakersfield until the 2022 announcement that the city would be getting a new Boot Barn location.

CHAPTER 13

NINETY-NINE THINGS

Part of what I really took away from writing my P's & Q blog during COVID was learning the power of a self-dare. The gentler way to refer to this idea is probably by calling it "challenging yourself," which is essentially what it was. Few of us accomplish much without pushing ourselves beyond our comfort zones and asking a little more than the status quo from ourselves.

But there is a subtle difference, I think, between goal-setting and a self-dare. Setting a goal means you have a particular destination and you are putting down a marker and saying you're going to get there.

For example, writing this book was a goal of mine. It was something I had the strong sense I should do while I was in the process of writing the blog. And when I wrapped up the blog, I set a goal to write a book. Of course, that target date moved and morphed a few times, but eventually, I got there.

And that is where I think a self-dare is a little different. Because for me, anyway, it's more about the immediate process than a long-range destination. *Hey, I bet you can't write a blog post every day* said the voice in my head (Hi, Carl). When I had days where I desperately didn't feel like writing a post, I'd hear that negative voice laughing, saying *See?*

Well, I wasn't giving that voice satisfaction. As I approached my 100th consecutive blog post, I felt like trying to mark the occasion in a special way. Not knowing what that would look like and feeling kind of intimidated about what to write for number 100, I came up with a goofy idea for my 99th post. The idea that popped in my head was *How about I just write 99 things I've learned so far in the pandemic?*

At first, I tried thoughtfully crafting that list. Then I realized how many things 99 is. I also got super busy doing whatever else I needed to do as a functioning human being and parent that night.

What ended up happening was that I stood at my kitchen counter, waiting for dinner to wrap up in the oven, and wrote this "99 Things" post in one frantic sitting. As a writing approach, it was outside my normal zone of comfort. I just decided to dive in, push through, and dare myself to get to 99.

I did somehow get to 99, which I have to emphasize once again, is a lot of things. It's amazing what you can accomplish when you have an annoying negative voice inside that you are dedicated to proving wrong. Thank you, Carl. This one's for you.

As a snapshot of that moment in time, here's what I wrote for that 99th post:

Day 99: Ninety-Nine Things
by Jim Schneider | Jun 24, 2020

As I was about to make dinner, I looked up at my usual prep station in the kitchen and saw a lovely piece of undersea artwork that Amelia made for me earlier this year. She wanted to put it somewhere that I would see it and it would make me smile, so we decided on this little patch of wall near the stove.

At the time, I probably expected to leave it up there for a few days. This drawing went up pre-quarantine. I think sometime in February. I do look at it when I cook, and it does make me smile.

That said, when I looked at it today, I realized that it had become such a fundamental part of the kitchen, like the stove or refrigerator, I wasn't actively noticing it anymore. Like so many things in our lives, it fell off my radar even though it was right in front of my face.

The memory of putting it up was a little surreal because it wasn't all that long ago, but it might as well have been a lifetime ago. It was at a different time when we had dreamed and thought about doing things that never came to pass.

I'm sure I'm not alone in feeling like I've aged way more than 99 days since this whole thing started, but this is my 99th blog post, so I thought I'd share 99 things I've observed in quarantine. Much like this blog itself, this post is starting off as a dare against myself. I have no idea if I'll come up with 99. But here I go.

1. It is hard to type with a four-year-old holding onto your left arm.
2. It is hard to type with a four-year-old holding onto your right arm.
3. Even when you don't really drive anywhere because the world is shut down, it turns out vehicle registrations still expire.
4. Toilet paper is never, ever to be taken for granted again.
5. Paper products in general are not to be taken for granted.
6. Disinfecting wipes are precious.
7. Strange things become scarce when people start hoarding. For example, every Whole Foods I visited for almost a month was consistently cleaned out of pizza sauce.
8. I always liked personal space in public. I like it much more now.

9. It's possible to feel claustrophobic in wide open areas.

10. Zoom is pretty awesome.

11. The mute button on Zoom is very important.

12. Cannellini beans are good and handy, but there is no disaster that would necessitate having more than four cans of them.

13. When hoarding, frozen vegetables are very handy and can be used in lots of things.

14. Bidets are pretty cool.

15. Even I can install a bidet. (This might be the most surprising revelation here.)

16. School is extremely important to kids.

17. School is extremely important to adults.

18. Being able to work from home is a blessing.

19. Working from home can also be extremely challenging.

20. Distractions can really—Hey, put that down!!!

21. When everyone has dogs and kids in the background during conference calls, the overall embarrassment level drops.

22. Still, my son can really shout into a call like few others.

23. My son has got some pipes, let me tell you.

24. Norfolk terriers are adorable and loving little dogs.

25. When it comes to bark volume from dogs, size matters not. Their weight-to-noise ratio is shocking.

26. For a suburban dad in his mid-forties, celebrating St. Patrick's Day in quarantine is exactly the same as celebrating it before quarantine.

27. Explaining a viral pandemic to small children is extremely difficult.

28. Kids are stronger and more adaptable than I ever could have imagined.

29. Adults can also be strong and adaptable when conditions warrant.

30. Boxes make great spaceships, cars, or whatever the imagination conjures.
31. Kids' imaginations are delightful and inspiring.
32. I believe adults can still access that imagination.
33. Playing make believe with kids is awesome and everyone should try it.
34. One of the things that motivates me each day is wondering what the kids will come up with next.
35. I miss being with people.
36. I particularly miss friends and family.
37. That said, I couldn't have possibly picked three better people to be in quarantine with. I am very fortunate.
38. My wife is amazing and quite literally keeps me sane.
39. Wait, that was two things . . .
40. My wife is amazing . . .
41. . . . AND keeps me sane.
42. Ninety-nine is a big number to assign to a list.
43. Ninety-nine is probably not an unusual number of items on my earlier, hoard-heavy Trader Joe's lists.
44. I am very bad at LEGOs.
45. I often lack the will to put down a Draw Four on my kids when playing UNO.
46. I need a much bigger office to properly display all the artwork the kids have made for me.
47. Backyard sprinklers are simple, wonderful, and fun.
48. The stubborn willpower of kids who want a snack is the most powerful force in the universe.
49. The stubborn willpower of kids who want to watch a particular cartoon is the second most powerful force in the universe.
50. Contrary to what comic books taught me, a big common threat like aliens or a pandemic won't bring people together.

51. People can be unbelievably shortsighted and petty.
52. People can also be kind, strong, resilient, and amazing.
53. I have to believe that number 52 outweighs number 51.
54. We are living through history.
55. Future generations will not be bored when their teachers get into the lesson about 2020.
56. Nothing good comes without challenge, and we are in a time of supreme challenge.
57. The optimist in me believes that this means there are truly great days ahead.
58. The pessimist in me has a hard time seeing how we get there.
59. I call the pessimist in me Carl.
60. I spend a good deal of time telling Carl to suck it.
61. Carl sounds like Tim Curry in *The Hunt for Red October*.
62. I miss going to restaurants.
63. I miss going out with my wife.
64. I really miss taking the kids to the grocery store with me.
65. I miss taking them to places like the children's museum, and I wonder when or if I'll get to do that again.
66. Buying an annual pass to the children's museum in January was probably not a terribly good investment this year.
67. But seriously, it was a great investment, and I should probably find a way to donate more because those guys are great and the kids love it there.
68. The kids stopped asking when they can go to the children's museum in early April.
69. We all miss taking trips together.
70. I don't miss doing a lot of work travel, but . . .
71. . . . it is weird not having been to the airport in months.
72. I bet my smooth routine getting through security would be all messed up and rusty now.

73. I don't think I'll be getting Premier Status on United this year.
74. For the first time in my life, I'm kind of nervous about flying.
75. I am very thankful to live in a state with lots of beautiful things to see within driving distance.
76. This blog has reminded me that I love writing.
77. That might seem obvious because I write a lot here, but I wasn't sure for a lot of years.
78. You can like writing, and still overdo it by daring yourself to write a list of 99 things on any topic.
79. My original idea was to riff something off the song "99 Luftballons," but holy cow that song is long and complicated.
80. Dares can also be good. I dared myself to write this blog every day and I've somehow managed to do it for 99 days.
81. It makes me think of George McFly saying, "If you put your mind to it, you can accomplish anything."
82. It's been fun watching some movies during quarantine.
83. *Back to the Future* is a nearly flawless movie.
84. *The Princess Bride* is a flawless movie.
85. *Robin Hood: Prince of Thieves* is a . . . flaw-full movie. Or "flawful?" Is that a word?
86. I'm inventing the word "flawful" right now.
87. I am sincerely enjoying some new reboots of classic cartoons that the kids are into.
88. The Amazon Prime *New Adventures of Rocky and Bullwinkle* is super silly and fun.
89. The movie *Scoob* is surprisingly good.
90. Amelia has been watching the new *She-Ra and the Princesses of Power* on Netflix and it is quite good.
91. I couldn't be more proud of my kids.

92. I couldn't be luckier than to be raising them with Erin.
93. We have a big job teaching them about love and justice in the world.
94. We all have a part to play in making a better world for our kids.
95. I look forward to quieter and better days.
96. I look forward to having a fresh draft beer again.
97. I look forward to traveling again.
98. I look forward to seeing you in person again.
99. I am very, very, very thankful to everyone who reads this blog. It helps keep me going. And if you made it all this way, I think I owe you a tote bag or something.

CHAPTER 14

CRUEL SUMMER

Being a parent means flying by the seat of your pants. Every day, new challenges are put before us and we are forced to react. Life is full of that kind of thing anyway, but with little kids around, adults have the added pressure of having to at least appear steady, confident, and knowledgeable.

This is hard enough to accomplish on any given day. Countless are the instances I've had to explain to the kids why they can't eat a potato-chips-only diet or why it's important to floss. The reality is that I would absolutely love to subsist on chips and dip. And I strongly agree that flossing sucks.

The year 2020 presented so many challenges, unique to my time as a parent. How do you explain a scary pandemic to young kids in terms that both communicates the severity of the threat while also providing the reassurance that children need? How could we tell our kids that people were dying and this is serious enough to account for the fact that we couldn't go out and do fun things without filling their minds with images of fear, pestilence, and death?

As a Gen-Xer and child of the 1980s, I feel a lot of pressure as a parent to communicate effectively with my kids and not pass on the angst and cynicism that so many of us carry. I have been in a lifelong struggle with worry and pessimism. I'm sure that comes from lots of different places, but I suspect being brought up in a time when the Russians were threatening the use of nuclear weapons couldn't have helped. Thank goodness we don't have to worry about that anymore.

The fact that I can remember being single-digit years of age and having an internal dialogue about whether it would be better to be near ground zero and vaporized or go on to live in a radiated nuclear winter probably speaks volumes for my overall sense of mental well-being.

Striking the balance with COVID was hard. But during the first few months, we all at least had the luxury of a general consciousness focused enough on this problem to keep everyone on kind of the same page. Of course, that didn't last. Long preexisting divisions and societal strain started quickly enough with pressures from lockdown.

And then came George Floyd.

On May 25, 2020, George Floyd was killed by a police officer in Minneapolis. The video of the horrific event went viral, and the nation—already on the brink, stressed by years of political division and months of pandemic—saw the gut-wrenching image of a police officer kneeling on a man's neck until the breath went out of him.

Our kids were young at the time and weren't plugged in to the news or daily events. They didn't see this roll out in real time. I felt awful for parents of older children, old enough to actually see and digest what was happening in real time. How in the world can you explain something like that? Helping our kids understand horror and injustice is one of the toughest parts of the parenting job.

Erin and I knew even then that we couldn't and shouldn't shield our kids from it. Because this is a reality that is much, much bigger than any of us. We can't teach them about the ideals humanity strives for without talking to them about the terrible failures we experience along the way.

I struggled—and continue to struggle—because, aforementioned pessimism aside, I have spent most of my life wanting to believe in the inherent goodness of humanity. But it is impossible to deny that there are strong winds of injustice always blowing in the face of progress. At that moment in time, I felt that it was clear that we needed to acknowledge the poison of racism and do something about it. All of us.

Sadly, what happened in Minneapolis wasn't a new story. Even though it briefly felt like a "never-again" moment, it sure hasn't played out that way. But it was a clarifying moment where many of us realized that we must do our part to advocate for and fight institutional racism and injustice in our society. I know that it inspired a lot of parents, of all backgrounds and colors, to think more about how we raise our children to live in an equitable world.

Of course, so much of that is what we as parents model for them, what we teach them, and how we talk about the issue of race. It isn't enough for kids to simply learn to treat everyone equally. Yes, that is the foundational idea, but there is more to it than that. Kids also need to understand that not everyone shares that view, which means that those who believe in equity have to work harder to advocate together for everyone if true equality is to ever happen.

Erin and I spent a lot of time discussing how to approach it. How do we teach our kids about this? How can we communicate the value of justice and equity in a positive way while also making them aware that bad things can and do happen? How can we stare down something this ugly while instilling in them the will and faith to make a better world for the future?

I think being honest about discrimination and oppression, both in the past and present, is very important. No, I do not think that teaching our kids about the history of racism in this country and pointing out the small and large ways that people of color face challenges even today is "making kids feel bad about themselves." Maybe it's because I myself have been a history nerd ever since childhood. I think it's important for all of us, kids and adults, to understand that history is made up of a patchwork of narratives and points of view. History is not always cuddly or pretty. In fact, it is almost always ugly, complicated and thorny.

It's not only possible, but healthy for us to look at our own nation's past and be both proud of our story while understanding that we don't always get it right. In fact, it isn't just that we don't always get it right. Sometimes we get it really, *really* wrong. That's not pride versus shame, that's a little thing called "nuance" that I think is really lacking in the national dialogue these days.

Thinking about that also meant taking a hard look at myself. I'm a middle-aged white guy who has had it reasonably easy compared to many others, so I know I'm the last person anyone needs to hear from on this topic. But I am a participant in society, and I would much rather make a positive than negative impact. It is my job to listen, learn, and advocate the best that I can. Part of that for me personally is acknowledging my own failures.

I generally think I am a decent, well-meaning person, but that doesn't make me perfect. The biggest epiphany I had during the dawn of the Black Lives Matter movement was so embarrassingly simple, I am almost ashamed to write it. To put it plainly: me simply not being outwardly, aggressively racist is not enough. And the hard truth is, that is probably the fallacy I've operated under for a long time.

Yes, doing our best to treat people fairly and equally is great, and clearly an important step. But it's not enough. Because that means we're not stopping to understand the challenges that people of color or individuals in other disadvantaged communities go through every day at the hands of those who don't take that very basic first step. It also means not standing up and advocating when the moment calls.

And here is where I know I have failed. I have been a part of conversations, meetings, and interactions where people made racist comments, and I let them stand because I didn't want to get into an argument. I am a generally nonconfrontational person, so I allowed myself to think it was OK to just walk away, because I didn't want to rock the boat. And hey, *I* didn't say it, so it's not my fault, right? In the end, those were excuses and not acceptable—and not something I'd want my kids to do.

I knew when George Floyd died, his death would fall into the usual groove of becoming a political issue in this country. Because everything does. Climate change, health, gun safety, and even COVID-19 have all been used to deepen political divisions—law enforcement reform and addressing institutional racism has, too.

But here's the thing, it should not be that way. This should not be an issue that divides us. It should bring us together. This is a basic issue of human decency and respect. I don't care who you vote for or what you believe, we should all be able to agree to basic fairness and the fact that no one should have to fear for their or their children's lives on a daily basis.

I remember the days of protests following George Floyd's murder, there was a heartbreaking video making the rounds on social media that showed three generations of Black men at a protest. They were expressing their frustration about having to keep coming back to this emotionally charged injustice over and over and over again. A man in his thirties, nearly in tears, plead passionately with a younger man in his teens, saying that it's up to the younger generations to find a better way, because the way we've been doing it isn't working.

He's right. It's not working. But it shouldn't only be up to the younger generations to save us. We all need to do better than that. So please, let's learn, listen, and reflect. In my humble opinion, one important first step is just opening your world to different perspectives. The first thing we need to do as parents is educate ourselves so we can educate our kids.

Follow diverse voices on social media. Read books and articles written by authors of color, or by members of the LGBTQIA+ or disability communities. Learn and absorb the difficult history of nonwhite communities so you can better understand the current reality of others. If you don't live in a diverse neighborhood, make a point to visit and explore ones that are with your kids so they can experience and understand different people and things. By taking in a diversity of voices and being open to different points of view, it's possible to learn a great deal by osmosis. It's not the end, of course, but it is a start, and more understanding and empathy is always a good thing.

All of us certainly have a lot of work to do to build a more equitable world, but I think listening and learning is foundational. It's not hard, and all of us can do it. Talk to your kids and encourage them to value other points of view, too. Be honest. Just starting the conversation is important. Even if it's difficult and clumsy, we all need to do it.

Our kids deserve a much better world than this. I know they are superheroes, but we shouldn't rely on them to save the day. We need to put on our capes, too.

Entering a global pandemic, I would have thought that the primary lessons we would have been faced with would have consisted largely of courses in epidemiology and which disinfectants work best. But life doesn't stop just because there is one big, rapidly spreading viral problem in front of us. It may have felt that way briefly, but the other normal currents in society and in our own individual lives just kept on churning. Good and bad things happen, and we have to interact and deal with those at any time, convenient or not.

I think May 25, 2020, was a shared experience that many of us briefly thought could bring unity and harmony. I thought *Surely this time there will be an appetite for real reform.* Instead, like the pandemic itself, sadly it became another dividing line for our society. That doesn't mean we stop trying. We owe it to our kids to keep striving for a better future.

COVID required all of us, certainly parents, to get pretty good at walking and chewing gum at the same time. Post-COVID, we are still all faced with many simultaneous challenges and still need to hone that skill. I will end by saying I am using that cliché here because everyone knows it and knows what it means, but seriously, have you ever met anyone who is NOT able to walk and chew gum at the same time? That is a pretty low bar to set. I think we can do it.

CHAPTER 15

WEIGHT, WEIGHT DON'T TELL ME

Like many, I was not my fittest self for much of 2020. Mentally and physically, I probably was what most doctors would call "a wreck."

My anxiety was through the roof, with depression also hanging around, and I may have partaken in a little stress eating. I'm probably alone on this. I know it's hard to believe anyone would want to stuff their face with pasta, chocolate, and other comfort food just because a scary disease was running rampant, my family had been in quarantine for months, the kids could barely leave the house, there was civil unrest, the economy was crumbling, *and* Jay Cutler and Kristin Cavallari broke up.

I mean, 2020 was a year of surprises, but I sure didn't see that one coming.

I would raid the pantry with all the enthusiasm and gusto of Sir Francis Drake looting a fleet of Spanish ships. There were no prisoners, and no safe quarter for the dried goods in my sight. My pirate's booty was crackers, chips, nuts and, on occasion, Pirate's Booty.

Oddly enough, I never touched all those cans of cannellini beans.

Suffice to say, I wasn't doing the greatest job of taking care of myself. Packing on "the quarantine fifteen" was an outward sign and I noticed my Before Time clothes, from back in the days when I used to wear lots of shirts with buttons instead of tees and sweatpants, were getting a little snug. I went from moving out a belt hole or two to simply realizing *Who needs belts anyway?*

But the weight gain was a symptom of a bigger holistic issue I was having. It reflected the fact that I wasn't feeling good inside or out.

The pandemic was a really difficult time for everyone, and Erin and I were no exception. She was struggling in her own way, too. The winds of life had forced her to shelve her plans to start a health coaching business, and she now was constantly on the phone or online trying to find help for Henry. We both wrestled with the difficulty of keeping Amelia engaged in rudimentary online school, and with finding ways to keep Henry occupied each day. Both of us were overwhelmed trying to keep our kids happy and healthy, and we found ourselves sinking as a result.

As adults, and parents especially, we tend to ignore our own needs and run ourselves into the ground for our jobs, our families, our friends, or whatever it might be. Parents tend to think they're not doing the job right if they aren't sacrificing their own well-being to put every ounce of energy toward their children.

I'm as guilty as anyone on this front and am notorious for pushing myself too hard—burning the candle at both ends, in the middle, and anywhere else. I was certainly wearing myself way too thin (not in the waistband) in those days and feeling the aftereffects. I was worn out, glum, irritable, and having difficulty being my best self.

Erin, too, was pushing herself entirely too hard and stressing out about our making the right decisions for Henry. There were so many choices and so much to sort through, and everything moved at a glacial pace. Erin is a problem-solver and someone who wants to get things done, which is a trait that can clash severely with a health care system seemingly designed to run you in circles and make you jump through infinite hoops. It can feel like playing a game of Chutes and Ladders, where you think you're near the end and you land on a space that sends you right back to the beginning.

There were times it felt like we were both so busy fighting our own battles each day that we weren't spending the time to connect back with each other. For us, it took mutual recognition of our personal struggles and taking active steps to come back to the center. That meant each of us finding ways to support ourselves as individuals and as a couple.

I am thankful for my wife for many reasons, and she was an enormous help to me and to us during this time. She knows me and is able to call me out on my stuff. I can be one who doesn't really accept or admit I'm struggling. In swimming terms, I could be treading water 100 feet out from shore and telling everyone, "I got this." Erin would say, "Hey, you're right by the shark rope," and help bring me back to shore. Her training as a health coach taught her many things about holistic well-being, and one of those things was the importance of self-care.

We hear the term "self-care" more commonly now, and it is an excruciatingly simple concept. It's care, but for YOURSELF! See how that works? Novel idea, right? So why is it so difficult?

Our culture seems to encourage this rather unhealthy take on "selflessness" to the degree that this is some martyr virtue in acting only for the well-being of others, and never yourself. It's somehow selfish to care for yourself, because clearly there is something else you could be doing. That is certainly implied in the Wisconsin small town culture I grew up in. Not only should you not put your own oxygen mask on first, you should make sure everyone else in the plane has theirs on AND has a nice casserole or assorted cheese platter before you put your mask on.

Of course, it's great to help and care for others. I think it's extremely important. But the nuance is that doing good for others doesn't mean ignoring your own needs.

As parents, many of us are especially susceptible to this kind of societal pressure. We are always supposed to be "on" for our kids first, and ourselves dead last. I certainly feel that, and I know that very often for moms it's exponentially worse. Moms are always supposed to leave it all on the field for their families, and Erin has long felt that pressure too. The pandemic, with all its stresses and challenges, was a time that taught us both that we simply can't be at our best, or even *third* best, if we don't care for ourselves.

When we were facing COVID, caring for and supporting our kids and everything else in that crucible summer of 2020, Erin and I both made a point to encourage each other to practice self-care and be kind to ourselves. A truly vital piece of perspective I learned from her was that self-care doesn't have to be a big, showy thing. Sure, it's great to take a trip or have a spa day or do something big from time to time. But on a day-to-day basis, self-care can be as simple as taking a little time to take a walk or go out for a cup of coffee and read for an hour.

Little things mean a lot. Like habit building, doing a little something positive for yourself each day can start very small, yet have a huge impact. That was such an important lesson for me to learn, and it's something all parents should try. I know we all feel like the days are too full already and there can't possibly be time to do anything for ourselves. But if you make a point to schedule something, even if it's fifteen minutes for a little meditation or time outside, it truly makes a difference. And it becomes a habit.

Taking the pressure off myself, realizing that self-care didn't have to be a huge undertaking, helped me manage and make actual progress. As an example, I have been a pretty regular runner for years, but I was really getting down on myself during lockdown because my pace and distance were down, and I wasn't hitting it as hard as I used to. Erin helped me realize that things like pace and distance can be goals, for sure, but it's not the *point*. The point is getting some movement—and movement of any kind is better than no movement.

So, I took the pressure off myself, got rid of the stopwatch and distance tracker, and just started running without worrying about it. Now, with running back in my routine every morning, I'm not focused on the stats. I'm focused on the fresh air, the sunshine, and doing this little thing for myself at the start of my day.

Likewise, I supported Erin taking time for herself, to take walks, get out, and take breaks to do the things that she enjoys. She loves to read, journal, and go for hikes with our dogs. It's important for parents, no matter their situation, to make the effort to find ways to support themselves outside of their children.

I know society has taught us that as parents we're supposed to sacrifice everything for our kids. Of course, there is nothing we wouldn't do for our kids, but how effective can we be if we aren't at our best, too? To be our best as parents, we also have to foster our health and growth as individuals.

This is an area that Erin and I have worked very hard on during the past few years—understanding that to best support each other and our children, we need to have the space to care for ourselves. We have our time, activities, and goals as a family, but we all each have our own individual things, too.

Erin is an entrepreneur and puts her heart and soul into building and growing her business. I love that about her and do my best to encourage and cheer her on at every step. Building a business is not easy, and it's particularly challenging to get yourself out there during a pandemic. She really did create a new form of service from scratch, and worked hard to pave a path and, to borrow a phrase from *Star Trek*, boldly go where no one has gone before. That meant moments of great excitement when she would sign a new client or line up a speaking engagement, but also moments of frustration and disappointment when she'd hit a roadblock or a prospect wouldn't sign up.

I am a writer, and for years I merely dabbled. I always *meant* to write a book or a screenplay and would do a little bit here and there. But Erin finally encouraged me to take concrete steps, build a schedule, and connect with professionals who would help me. Writing and publishing this book has been a longtime goal for me, and her support of this part of my personal growth journey has been vital to the process. But as with Erin's business, I had moments of feeling great when I thought things were coming together, and also times where I'd get so frustrated or lost in the process that I wanted to burn my hard drive, bury it, and salt the land over it so nothing of this book would ever grow again.

What I think we both learned along the way is that supporting a loved one is not the same as fixing things for them. When Erin would hit those potholes in business, I had to accept that there wasn't anything I could do to fix it, nor should I. I just tried to listen, be there, and offer the love and support I could.

Erin taught me that, because she also would feel that way when I would get discouraged about my writing, or my job, or anything else in my sphere. I'm not asking anyone to fix any of that, but it sure does feel nice to be heard and seen. So we learned to ask each other what we need in a given moment, whether that's advice, reinforcement, or just a loving ear. Clarifying that has gone a long way in our helping each other on our individual journeys.

It's hard to know exactly what life would look like had COVID not come around—and I still sure wish it hadn't—but I also can't deny that facing what we faced made Erin and I stronger as a couple and as individuals. Adversity can do that. And for all the difficulty of the year 2020, I am thankful for what we learned together.

To parents out there, no matter what your situation, I encourage you to commit to taking care of yourselves. It can start small. Take fifteen or thirty minutes each day to do something for yourself. Take a walk, take a bath, read, or indulge in a trashy TV show. **Put it on**

your calendar. Schedule it. If you're like me and you don't make a point to physically schedule it, it probably won't happen.

If you have a partner, be sure to foster both your connection as a couple while also encouraging each other to grow individually. That means making time for yourself as an individual, and yourselves as a couple. Challenge your partner to join you in the self-care endeavor. Be accountable for each other and make sure you are each doing something to recharge every day.

If you're a single parent, find moments for yourself to care for you, the person. Not just you, the parent. It can be when the kids are at school or asleep—again, even fifteen minutes helps. Don't overwhelm yourself by trying to go big right away. You'll find that even blocking out a little time for mediation, a walk, a workout, journaling, or whatever makes you feel good can help.

Remember, you are more than a "parent." You are also *you*. Don't lose sight of what makes you who you are. If you put a little effort into nurturing yourself as an individual, it's amazing how much better you'll feel. And the healthier and stronger you are as an individual, the better you'll be as a parent, too.

And healthy means more than just the circumference of your waistband. During the pandemic, I may have started off my journey toward overall wellbeing a little overly fixated on the scale, but in time I came to understand that was just part of a larger whole. That said, with the help of calorie tracking, cleaner eating, regular running and cutting out the late-night pantry raids, I was able to shrink that literal "larger whole" to a somewhat smaller version. More importantly, I was able to shift my mentality toward recognizing that many small but meaningful pieces make up who we are, and each piece requires attention and care. I learned that a well-cared for spirit and mind goes a long way toward being my best self.

DO YOU REMEMBER?

The baking craze? With everyone all around the world suddenly cooped up at home, fending off boredom, there was a sudden and dramatic trend in baking.

There was the sourdough-starter craze that was all over social media, and studies showed that people were gravitating to lots of old-time comfort food. One artisanal flour mill in England reported a 500-percent increase flour demand. That type of shift, of course, led to shortages.

It's possible that this carb-heavy fad was in some way connected to another phenomenon that many of us dubbed "The Quarantine Fifteen."

CHAPTER 16

MY HEART

It was day 199 of COVID lockdown. October 1, 2020. It was a Thursday and a pretty busy day. Erin was out of the house taking our dog to the groomer. Henry's therapist couldn't make it, so it was like old times with me working and Henry hanging out nearby. Amelia was doing virtual school in her bedroom.

It's always a precarious balancing act—the whole working while looking after kids thing. It went OK, but there were definitely some challenges. Mainly that you have to learn to work in between the random interruptions every few minutes. Even when there is a moment of peace, you're running the clock in your head for the next snack request or random shouting.

For any fellow science fiction nerds reading this, it reminds me of "33," the first full episode of the *Battlestar Galactica* reboot that aired back in the mid-2000s. In that episode, the crew was haggard and worn because every thirty-three minutes, their enemies—the dreaded android Cylons—would appear and attack. Every. Thirty-three. Minutes.

When the episode begins, this pattern had been going on for many days, and everyone was on the edge of collapse. Now, while a child needing something or having a difficult moment *clearly* isn't nearly as stressful or serious as a sudden attack by killer space robots, the similarity is that you can never exactly lower your guard and settle your mind to other tasks.

And this was one of those days. Henry had some spicy moments, getting upset about this or that, and Amelia had a few technological issues with school. I remember one interruption occurred during Amelia's independent study time for art. I got her set up doing something with "Mo Willems Lunch Doodles." I was in my office, two rings into a phone call, when I heard an urgent yell, "Daddy! Daddy!"

I hung up the phone immediately and ran into Amelia's room, ready to deal with another distance-learning breakdown or other emergency. I got there and she looked at me, excited, and said, "Dad! Did you know that *Don't Let the Pigeon Drive the Bus* was Mo Willems' first book?!"

I did not know that.

I was equal parts irritated and impressed. Irritated about the interruption but impressed that my daughter has the same passion for trivia that I do.

After work, I succumbed to the repeated "Dad, can we go to the park?!" requests and decided to take them to a place we call "The Tunnel Park." It's about a mile away and has an actual name, but it also has these cool tunnels the kids love to run through, thus the nickname.

It was a beautiful day, and I had a hunch we'd have to work harder to navigate crowds than we had to last time we went when it was drizzling. Indeed, we arrived and saw a few groups of kids at the park, so we all masked up and proceeded with caution.

As time went on in the pandemic, we got more comfortable being outside unmasked. In fact, looking back on my writing about this day, it struck me how extremely cautious we were still being at a point in the pandemic when lots of people were throwing up their hands.

Stepping into my mindset of that time, we were still definitely within the zone of time where we were nervous about the kids getting sick, especially given Henry's sometimes unreliable immune system. Looking back, sure, maybe I'd do a few things differently. But I also give a lot of grace to my past self simply because there was so much we didn't know. This was all made easier by the fact that Amelia and Henry were both always fine wearing masks anyway, so we all preferred to play it safe.

When we got to the park, there was a small group of parents off to the side, and a herd of unmasked, feral-looking boys running all around in a herd. There was definitely a Neverland-Lost-Boys-from-the-movie-*Hook* vibe going on, but we figured we'd give it a shot and try to find our own spaces to play in.

It amounted to the kids and me playing in an area for a while until the herd came running back, and then we'd distance ourselves and go somewhere else. It was tricky, but I have to say the kids were quite adept at it, doing the distancing automatically, really.

I felt relieved, because I wanted them to be staying safe. Yes, it was surreal and sad to realize that this whole creating space thing had become such a part of their lives that my kids now naturally keep their distance from people.

We did the best we could, and the toughest part came when a little boy, maybe about five, started hanging around close to my kids. Like the others, he was unmasked, but he clearly was both part of and not part of that group. He was very sweet, but I got a little nervous because I wanted to keep my kids safe. I found myself kind of running block and making sure they stayed at least a few feet away.

Before COVID, Amelia would take great pride in the fact that she would make a new friend almost every time we went to the playground. And I saw her struggling with that urge as the boy parallel played with them. I was looking after Henry, and the little boy was near Amelia, and I could hear them start to talk.

Amelia introduced herself, and so did he. We were about to head over to this rope-bridge-climbing thing, and Amelia told him about it. I started toward them to try to make sure they were standing some distance apart, and I heard the little boy say, "My mom says I'm not supposed to play on that because it is too much for my heart."

And ladies and gentlemen, that was too much for *my* heart.

This little boy was just looking for connection with my kids and to have fun as best he could too—and here I was feeling nervous about that. It tore me up inside. In what felt like a safety concession to me at that moment, I had a talk with the kids and told them it was OK to play with the little boy, just try to play it safe as possible.

Henry and Amelia and the little boy chased around a little and played hide-and-seek. The whole time, I both fretted because I wanted to make sure I kept the kids healthy and felt deeply sad that I even had to let my mind go there. The more I watched this little boy, the more I wondered if maybe the little boy was autistic or had special needs like Henry. The group he was there with was clearly pretty rough-and-tumble, and he was on his own. I was glad he got to have his own fun with Amelia and Henry.

This was maybe the first time I realized that all these restrictions and precautions that had been drilled into all of us for months—especially the kids during a formative time in their lives—was going to leave a mark. I felt it in my own reticence of the kids playing with this little boy, and I saw it in the way my kids very smoothly and deftly kept a bit of a natural distance.

It also brings into focus something about Amelia that I admire so much. She is very often the one who finds that kid who isn't quite running with the rest of the crowd. She sees them, understands them, and values them. Maybe some of it comes from her experiences with Henry, but I think a lot of it is just who she is. I know it's a cliché thing to say that we learn from our kids, but I absolutely believe it, and this is something I admire very much about her. She could sense that this little boy needed to be seen that day, and she saw him.

In the Before Times, Amelia would almost be disappointed if she left a playground or park without having made a new friend. But that hadn't been a thing in our realm of reality for quite a while. It moved me then—witnessing her big heart reaching for a little boy's bruised one—seeing it play out again. It gave me some confidence that although life had changed and I worried about long-term impacts, that part of her hadn't gone away.

After a little while, it was time to leave and they had to say goodbye to their new friend. We headed back home and got on with the rest of our evening. I was proud of my kids for many reasons. Proud that they wore masks without complaint and knew what to do to stay safe. I was proud that they always saw the special part of everyone they meet.

This little episode drove home how much this time was going to affect their entire generation. Having a chunk of their precious childhood where you had to avoid other human beings to stay healthy is probably going to have an impact on them. I don't think we can know yet what that means.

Maybe it'll be positive and they won't take human contact for granted, the way previous generations have. Or maybe it will create issues we don't understand yet. In the end, I guess I must have faith that we have done the best we can with the information we had each step of the way and just choose to think my kids will take something good from it. They always seem to.

There is also a lesson I took from this particular day-in-the-life episode, and a reason why I decided to include this story. When sitting down to write this book, I reviewed some old posts from the daily blog I kept for a year and a half, which is when I came across the Tunnel Park story. I can say, with great certainty, that I would have forgotten about this entire wonderful, adorable moment my kids experienced had I not written it down. When I was skimming my posts, I couldn't for the life of me remember what this one was, and it wasn't until I read the whole post that the memory came rushing back.

It makes me wonder what other beautiful moments I have forgotten in my life. I am at least appreciative to have this one back.

It taught me the importance of a written record. Journaling, even if it's just a few sentences a day, can help preserve these moments that can be so fleeting. The adage about how kids "grow up so fast" is absolutely true. As a sentimental sop of a parent, I try to hoard the special moments, like a miser—and writing things down is absolutely the best way to do that.

DO YOU REMEMBER?

Big Bird getting vaccinated for COVID-19? Since its launch in 1969, Sesame Street has dedicated itself to helping kids understand complicated issues and work through scary or difficult times. From Big Bird getting vaccinated for measles in 1972, to Mr. Hooper's death in 1983, to the time when Oscar the Grouch moved into a recycling bin, Sesame Street has always been there to inspire and encourage the nation's young children.

The beloved character's attempts to soothe kids' fear of getting the COVID vaccine, however, met with notable controversy. U.S. Senator Ted Cruz, a man with enormous responsibilities who chooses to spend his time attacking oversized children's puppets on social media, criticized as "government propaganda" the simple post from a make-believe bird, issued with the intent to make kids feel safe. Other conservatives derided the iconic TV bird's efforts as "evil" and "brainwashing."

While far from the first time that Sesame Street has drawn political ire, the rate of success on Big Bird attacks remains stunningly low. Most Americans have considerable affection for Big Bird and tend to stand with him, even if there was initially some skepticism of the existence of his best friend Mr. Snuffleupagus. People of all party affiliations now acknowledge the existence of Snuffy, though Mike Lindell has accused him of rigging voting machines.

CHAPTER 17

UNHOLY CHOICE

My college friends and I used to spend ridiculous amounts of time playing a game we called "Unholy Choice." Also known to many as "Would You Rather." It was basically each of us posing a series of equally horrifying scenarios and asking the others which they would choose.

For example, one of my all-time favorites was *Would you rather, for the duration of one year, wear clothes made only from steel wool, OR wear a costume of the McDonaldland character, Grimace, for that same year?*

With the Grimace costume, you could never tell anyone why you were wearing it. For example, any family event you had to attend—be it a funeral, wedding or birthday party—even though people would obviously stare at you in disgust and ask, "For god's sake, why are you wearing a giant purple Grimace costume?" you could only shrug and offer no explanation.

So, posed here is a pretty clear choice about what kind of pain you'd prefer to experience. Would you rather take the physical discomfort of wearing steel-wool clothes, or the mental and emotional trauma involved with becoming a pariah to all your loved ones for wearing nothing but a Grimace costume for twelve months?

Being a parent in the time of COVID felt an awful lot like playing a real-life version of Unholy Choice. We were all constantly faced with equally awful choices, not just for ourselves, but for our children, and we had to navigate them daily.

Do we choose crushing disappointment for our kids? Or potential infection for our kids? Both super fun options. Both have short-term consequences, whether that's screaming and crying or coughing and wheezing, as well as potential long-term consequences. In this case, that could be steeping bitterness for longing of childhood whimsy lost forever, or the lingering symptoms of long COVID.

This played out in so many ways during the pandemic. Unholy Choice draws included things like:

- Hey, one of the kids' birthdays is coming up! Our choices are:

    A. Stay bunkered in the house, having yet another box-mix cake and watch a movie.

       or . . .

    B. Have a proper birthday party and risk our kids, friends, and family getting long COVID!

- Hey! Our son has been diagnosed with autism! Our choices are:

    A. Stay bunkered in the house, isolated from all of humanity, including therapists and support professionals who can really help him.

       or . . .

    B. Get him working with excellent therapists who may also be viral vectors and once again . . . long COVID!

- Hey! My niece is graduating from high school and there is a family celebration back in Wisconsin! Our choices are:

    A. Stay bunkered at home, send a card, and eventually see a few pictures of the event, missing this special moment in the life of a dear family member.

       or . . .

B. Travel across the country through and to several COVID hotspots to celebrate, enjoy some human contact, and potentially, long COVID!

- Hey! I dislocated my toe because I fell down in the backyard while cleaning up dog poop! (Actual story.) My choices are:

    A. Stay bunkered up at home and away from the potential infection stew that is the local urgent care in the middle of a pandemic and just shove that toe back in myself.

    or ...

    B. Seek proper medical attention at the local urgent care, leading to a certain repair of my toe, with a side of potential long COVID.

Either way, we parents were always put squarely in the position of being, at best, a buzzkill, killjoy, or whatever the kids are saying these days. At worst, we could be in the position of making a regrettable health and safety decision. Either way, it didn't feel good. An unholy choice.

And while we erred on the side of extreme caution, we often did not. The answer key to the above scenarios was A, B, B, B. (Yes, I DID get my toe professionally reset.) We were fortunate to have made it through that period, even with taking some measured risks, without getting sick. Still, the unholy choice felt like something we were dealing with on a constant basis. It's stressful enough to be making big decisions for our family or our kids without also throwing two major factors into the mix: mortality and uncertainty.

We knew the virus was potentially deadly or debilitating. Where children were concerned, there were those who basically said that kids weren't getting infected at all, and others who were saying *Yeah, it's not super common. But if you do get it, oh boy, look out.* There were lots of horror stories of long COVID with lingering effects, like loss of focus and energy.

But how real a risk was it? I still feel like it's hard to assess. It was a real struggle for a guy like me, with one section of the brain being dominated by Mr. Spock-level statistically driven logic and the other section being ruled by panic-level anxiety reacting to the smallest of threats.

I read lots of articles and listened to lots of podcasts interviewing specialists and professionals, trying to understand how to make the best, safest decisions. From what was understood at the time, my and Erin's concern about potential child infection was that the chances of infection and serious illness was not zero. Rationally, I could look at data sets and see that the chances of problems for kids were low. But as parents thinking about the welfare of our two children, we had a hard time processing much that was above zero.

And there was the uncertainty. We know a lot more about COVID now than we did in spring and summer of 2020—which is an easy bar to clear because back then, we knew pretty much nothing about it. Back then, we had to make these calls with very little information and lots of fear. Looking back, I can see things I would have probably been more relaxed about if I knew what I know now. But I also don't regret making the choices we did at the time because we were operating with the best intentions and knowledge we had then.

One of the biggest unholy choices in 2020 and 2021 was around the issue of school. There was a constant push-pull of whether in-person school was safe or not. That's an issue that remains a point of contention, because there certainly were learning losses for many children associated with school closures.

We did keep the kids home doing virtual school in 2020, with all its ups and downs. As with other things, we tried our best to weigh that particular unholy choice and did the best we could.

By the time we reached the Fall of 2021, there was plenty of evidence, technique, and practice to show that with masking and basic precautions, schools could slide into an area of risk that was more acceptable to us, so the kids went back. Was a school a risk-free environment? No, but there is also the counterpoint of the fact that kids do need that in-person interaction that school offers, and virtual school was, at best, a temporary Band-Aid for most. This was an example for us to weigh the risks and benefits.

Life always presents us with unholy choices. During the height of the COVID pandemic, the choices were particularly cruel and unusual. As time went on, some choices got a little easier. But I'm sure I'm not alone hearing that tiny contrary voice in my head questioning *Is this safe?*

Unholy choices are certainly not unique to the years 2020 and 2021. That being said, if you chose the Grimace costume in the year 2020, most of us never left our homes anyway, so that would have worked out pretty well.

DO YOU REMEMBER?

The Russian vaccine? On August 11, 2020, Russian President Vladimir Putin announced that Russia had approved a coronavirus vaccine named "Sputnik V."

This momentous development from the country that gave us Chernobyl, mass poisoning of political dissidents, and the 19th century generated near nil demand of the vaccine from the rest of the world who, for the most part, decided to take their chances with the virus.

CHAPTER 18

EASTBOUND AND DOWN

In the Before Times, I took the kids grocery shopping with me almost every week. After COVID hit, that tradition stopped for months and months because we didn't feel it was safe for the kids to go out in public spaces. But as time went on, we began questioning many assumptions, including whether, indeed, Trader Joe's was a fecund swamp of disease or just a quirky grocery store.

A lot of parenting—and just being a living person in 2020, 2021, and beyond—was weighing risks and doing a lot of cost-benefit analysis about what constituted an acceptable risk. That kind of assessment eventually spurred Erin and I to stop and reassess the grocery store risk. So sure, if the kids wore a mask, they could certainly come to the store with me. By midsummer, we were way past the time of wiping down groceries and being worried about surface transmission, after all.

But we continued to weigh these kinds of decisions, considering them several times. And I am thankful for my wife for many reasons, but it was she who was able to see things more reasonably and counter my anxious paranoia, certainly throughout those early days of the pandemic.

The thing with considering risk and reward is that there is the whole "reward" part of the equation. Sometimes, it takes a little chance to get to the good stuff— that is what Erin was always so good at reminding me of. Myself, often an anxious scaredy cat, I tend to focus only on the "risk" part of that scenario and, left to my own devices, would probably have seldom left the house for most of 2020.

Each family had to find their own comfort zone and what constituted acceptable risk for that reward. Erin understood in the early days better than I did that the reward of getting out of the house was worth some level of risk to do things. One of the first examples was when she suggested making a day trip to Vail, Colorado, to take a walk and have lunch at one of our favorite restaurants for Father's Day.

I remember tepidly agreeing to that, then being super nervous about going up there. But we did it safely. We wore masks everywhere and ate well distanced from everyone at a table by a huge open door. It was wonderful and worth it.

After that came some larger leaps that we made from that first year of the pandemic. Once again, I credit Erin for seeing the clear path on this one. My niece was graduating from high school and having a party in July of 2020. We hadn't seen my family back in Wisconsin in quite some time, and Erin asked me if maybe we should go back for the graduation and see everyone.

Living as far away as we do, we don't make it back for a lot of those family events. And I admit, at the time, the question caught me a little off guard because I was still so focused on the "risk" part. But after we talked about it, we decided to give it a shot.

In no way were we ready to get on planes at that point, but our family is made up of experienced road trippers, so we packed up the car, charged the kids' tablets, and hit the road for a two-day trip back to Wisconsin.

We would usually stay in Nebraska around the halfway mark, and I remember being particularly stressed about this stop because we were still pretty nervous about hotels. We wiped everything down when we got in and wore masks in all the common areas. And overall, we felt we were doing as well as we could. Again, risk vs. reward.

Part of the reward just came with watching the kids in the hotel room. Being little kids, it doesn't matter where you're staying, being in a hotel room is **awesome**. They jumped back and forth between the beds and loved getting breakfast goodies from the convenience store downstairs.

The next morning, we were back in the car and on our way. As soon as we arrived, my focus shifted even more to the reward side, because it was really nice to see the family, with warm welcomes all around. The isolation of COVID was very difficult and constant, so those moments where we got to be with loved ones outside of a Zoom screen always felt extra special.

My niece had a great outdoor party and we at least got to see the immediate family and watch the kids spend time with grandma and grandpa. We stayed with my sister and her family and had a wonderful time just being around others again.

After that big trip, we did start to tiptoe out a little more, doing things like camping and taking some other small trips to get out of the house for a little while. Also on the radar was another trip back to Wisconsin, potentially over Labor Day weekend, for my brother's wedding in Milwaukee.

My brother and his fiancé were one of the many couples who had the misfortune of having a wedding planned during the early days of COVID, March of 2020, so it had to be postponed with all the early lockdowns.

They were able to schedule a scaled-back version of their wedding for early September. One thing I remember about that year is that, for whatever reason, a few months out always seemed like a safe move. *Things will be better by THEN, right?*

Of course, as a society, we haven't really had to deal with this kind of ongoing challenge and are used to things just wrapping up in a few months. Like TV seasons, problems like this are just supposed to end or go on hiatus.

But, waves, lulls, spikes, and valleys, COVID certainly hung around. Still, we were planning to attend the wedding and make another road trip back to Wisconsin. We'd done it safely once, we could do it again, right?

As we got closer to the wedding, there was a big COVID spike in Wisconsin. A lot of the Midwest was experiencing a surge, and several members of my family wound up coming down with the virus. Some mild, some more serious, but it was a shadow over the idea of going on this trip. And then, a couple weeks before, my mom tested positive.

Fortunately, she bounced back quickly and was clear before the wedding. But at the time, we had a serious debate about whether we should really make this trip. Risk versus reward, again. Erin and I talked about it quite a bit, and I even conferred with my brother about it. He was awesome and understanding and told everyone to do what was comfortable for them.

This felt like an example of high risk balanced against high reward. These decisions were always hardest when these two sides are in line. If it's high risk/low reward, it's easier. This is why I was often puzzled during outbreak spikes, when indoor dining was risky, to see packed parking lots at a TGI Fridays. No offense to Fridays, but that struck me as high risk, low reward. Their nachos are OK, but come on.

On the other hand, my brother's wedding was very important, and we really wanted to be there. We ultimately decided that the reward here was higher than the risk. So once again, we packed up the car and got ready to go eastbound.

There was another wrinkle going into this trip. We had gotten Henry's autism diagnosis back in April, and we had spent a couple months getting him set up for in-home therapy to help support him. In the end, this would pay amazing dividends, but by no means was it a straight line of progress. As many families of children with autism or other disabilities would tell you, those first few months of therapy can be hard—and things can go down before they go up.

Without going into massive detail, those early months are about learning more about how our son ticked and starting to help him work on things like self-soothing and communication. Until therapy, he spent his entire life finding workarounds, and frankly, so had we. Starting to mess with those well-worn tools and security blankets can create stress and conflict.

Henry's therapies started in July, and we immediately learned a lot about sensory tools, coping strategies, and ways to better communicate back and forth. There were days that were good and days where Henry would really struggle. The first few months had us all outside our comfort zone and struggling a little.

So that's where we were with Henry when my brother's wedding rolled around. At this point, I was still not talking about his identification as autistic in my blog, even though it was a big part of our everyday life. We had told our close family and a few friends about it, but I still wasn't sure how to talk about it.

Our therapy team gave us lots of strategies and frameworks to help us during our travels, and at the wedding itself. We took Henry to the Autism Store in Denver, a wonderful resource for families like ours. There we bought some cool sensory toys, like squeeze balls, fidgets, and stretchy things. Henry's occupational therapist worked with him to build a cool homemade glitter bottle that is kind of like looking at a lava lamp. We found that could also be an effective way to help Henry regulate and soothe in overwhelming moments.

We would see those strategies work, but he was still having trouble dealing with all the change that was happening during those first few months of therapy support. After all, he was four years old and suddenly dealing with all these new people in his life and shifting from being pretty much a free-range COVID-quarantined kid with his days wide open to now having structure and activities each day. It was a lot, and it was natural for him to push back sometimes. There would be days that felt like we were fighting over every little thing, and it was exhausting and challenging for all of us.

With the trip to Wisconsin coming up, we knew leaving the house and taking a trip could be stressful, and we wanted to do our best to prepare him. We went back to work trying to help Henry deal with different kinds of situations and environments. We consulted with his therapy team specifically to prep Henry for the journey and the event itself. I was going to be standing up in the wedding, so we wanted to help Henry understand what that means and coach him through the event in advance. We even did a mock wedding in the backyard so he could see how it would work and we could practice.

When we left for that trip, we felt as ready as we could be. We had several sensory toys, including the glitter bottle we made. Henry got quite good at requesting those tools when he needed them and would respond very well.

Henry is a good traveler, and he did great on the journey to Wisconsin. When we arrived, he was thrilled to see his grandparents and other relatives and had lots of fun playing around and exploring a new place.

The day of the wedding came, and we went over everything with Henry again. Erin had a bag with snacks and sensory toys ready for him. We were feeling good about things. There was just one red flag that gave us pause when we drove over to the venue for the ceremony: Henry rubbed his eyes when we got out of the car.

OK, he might be a little tired, but the ceremony is short, so we should be fine.

It was a small group, and Erin and the kids took their seats when it was time to begin. Henry was doing fine, watching his tablet. The venue was beautiful, and everything looked perfect. We started the procession and Henry saw me and wanted to come over to me.

That's where things started to go really, really wrong.

Erin tried all the snacks, toys, and everything else to settle him down, but Henry got fixated on wanting to run over to me. Before the bride even made it down the aisle, he erupted into what would be one of the toughest meltdowns he's ever had. In a totally new situation after long days of travel, he was off his footing. He couldn't understand why he couldn't just run up to me and couldn't process everything that was going on. Literally kicking and screaming, Erin had to grab him up and rush him out of the room as quickly as she could.

Amelia stayed behind by herself and sat perfectly through the rest of the ceremony. I felt awful that I couldn't help, and we all felt embarrassed for the interruption. The ceremony was beautiful, and Dave and Jess were wonderful. Unfortunately, Erin had to miss the entire thing because she was in the bathroom with Henry, struggling mightily to help him regulate.

In the end, Erin wound up driving around with Henry for a while, and we eventually took him back to the hotel to rest and calm down, while Amelia went to spend time with her grandparents.

This turned into a low point for us, and a major point of stress. Erin and I argued because I wanted to swoop in and help with Henry and she told me I should go with the wedding party for pictures. I stubbornly insisted on staying and helping and we were all really upset and stressed.

It's one of those moments I look back on and I don't feel great about how I handled it. My heart was in the right place, and I wanted to help Erin and Henry, but as a result, I wasn't there for my brother's wedding photos. Erin certainly could have handled things on her own. There *are* times as parents when we have to divide and conquer, but this time, my hero complex took over and I didn't assess the situation with a clear head.

But it was what it was. We muddled through that afternoon, frazzled, scared, hurt, and upset. We had looked forward to this and worked so hard for so many weeks and months to make it through that half-hour ceremony, and in the end, it went about as badly as we could ever have imagined.

That day, Erin and I both felt completely dispirited. It felt like all the effort, all the work, all the struggle and all the work we all had done had been for nothing. We wondered if this was just how it was going to be with Henry, all the time. Were we realistically going to be able to travel and do things like this? It's a low point that I think many parents who have autistic children, or children with other disabilities, experience.

All that said, Henry did regulate after getting some rest, and we were able to go back to the reception. As he often does after having an episode like that, he seemed truly tired and shaken. I know he doesn't like to have these meltdowns, either. They stress and exhaust him. People often talk about how difficult it is to handle a child having a meltdown, but it is so much more painful for the child experiencing it. I can't know how it feels inside, but I've heard autistic adults describe it as a burning sensation. It is painful. I know Henry doesn't want this to happen, and my heart breaks for him when it does.

He did well the rest of the night and we were able to enjoy the time with family, but the whole experience took us down a notch. We were tired and shell-shocked.

The next day, we headed back to Colorado laden with questions for our therapy team. In the end, we were glad we could be there for Dave and Jess, and the wedding was wonderful. But we found ourselves deeply questioning everything we were doing to help Henry. Was it even helping? What was the point of all this therapy when, in so many ways, it felt like he had actually gotten worse, not better?

Back home, I could feel the sadness and confusion from our team, as well. We had all put a lot into this, but what was the next step? We wondered whether we were using the right therapeutic plan. We wondered to ourselves whether he was just too inflexible to be able to handle different environments, worrying that travel with him was just going to be impossible.

That was the depth of the valley. But I can happily say we didn't stay there for very long. If you know anything about classic story structure, you understand that low points are also launching points.

The three-act structure is the backbone of most stories, and in that setup, the end of act two ends with the main character's low point. The point where all seems dark, hope seems lost, and the main character has to decide whether and how to fight on.

I knew enough from all the stories I've read and written that hope is never lost. The low point is where the hero or heroine learns who they are, what they're made of, and digs deep to fight on. And that is what our family did. It was a hard few weeks, I won't lie. Discouraging, difficult, and exhausting. But, spoiler alert: things *did* get better.

That fall, Henry started coming more and more into his own. His support team was amazing, and constantly impressed by how hard our son worked and the amazing progress he consistently made. He was learning more about how to manage his emotions and communicate to us when he needed help before he got to a point of no return. He now knew how to soothe himself and would advocate for himself when he needed to take a break and regulate. We helped give him the tools and—the amazing kid he is—he used them.

By spring of 2021, Henry was in pre-K and then kindergarten that fall, and he has continued to rock it. He probably has a higher emotional IQ and is better able to talk about how he is feeling than most adults I know. We are infinitely proud of him.

Looking back on that wedding day in September of 2020 is always a reminder to us of how far we have come. It is also something I readily share with any parent who is struggling. Hope is never lost, even if it might feel that way sometimes.

Henry still has meltdowns sometimes, sure. But now we know how to help guide him through it. We have a better idea of what can trigger issues and can work with him in advance to prepare him. Looking back on this, and knowing what we know now, we can understand that we threw way too much at him all at once. We should have built in more time and space for him to recover from the trip itself and built in more breaks. Of course, no one is perfect, there was a lot we didn't know, and we were so focused on trying to get through the trip without getting COVID that maybe a few other things got past us.

Now we know more ways to help Henry and set him up for success. But there is no point in getting caught up on what we could have done; instead, we've learned to be humble enough to pick up and learn from difficult moments.

That story is still being written, of course. He is six, almost seven right now, and we have a long path ahead. But in terms of risk/reward, I can look back on that wedding now and clearly see that the reward significantly outweighed the risk—not even close.

EXCERPT FROM JIM'S ABANDONED BOOK OF COVID KNOCK-KNOCK JOKES

Knock knock!
Who's there?
Vaccine passport.
Vaccine passport who?
Vaccine passports are banned in the states of Alabama, Arizona, Arkansas, Florida, Georgia, Idaho, Indiana, Iowa, Montana, North Dakota, South Carolina, South Dakota, Texas, and Wyoming, so don't tell this joke in those states.

CHAPTER 19

THE LET DOWN

The issue of kids and school during the pandemic is that it's a rare case when most parents—with different political stripes, backgrounds, and classes—can actually agree. It sucked.

To clarify, that statement is not a criticism of schools. I just happen to subscribe to the idea that sometimes in life, there are problems that just don't lend themselves to good solutions.

It's like if you're taking a long road trip through the middle of nowhere. You're starving, and your only food choices for the next 100 miles are a 7-Eleven with days-old microwave burritos or a thinly staffed Arby's located miles off any regular supply route. You have to make a choice, but either one will absolutely result in a stomachache.

March through May of 2020 were particularly brutal because there was just no time to prepare for an instant switch to virtual learning. Schools, teachers, parents, and students were all doing their best to find their way, but it was a crazed, shoot-from-the-hip affair at that point.

With a little more time to prepare for the next school year, districts were at least able to refine the process for the next school year. Where we live, with cases still very high over the summer, the district had decided to start the school year virtually and then transition to optional in-person learning.

We had been hoping for a hybrid model, which some districts were trying. This is where kids were in school a couple days a week and virtual on other days. It allowed greater opportunity for distancing and safety measures, but also got kids back into some in-person learning.

When I listened in on some district meetings over the summer of 2020, it was clear that the parents in the area fell into three camps: about 40 percent wanted full-time in-person learning, about 30 percent wanted all virtual, and another 30 percent wanted hybrid.

So, while a majority were not in favor of full-time back to school, the two camps making up that majority had slightly smaller numbers than the camp wanting full-time in person. It's the kind of goofy numbers trick that is unfortunately common in our society these days.

The school year started all virtual in August, with the idea that the district would reassess COVID levels after a few weeks and decide for the rest of the semester. We felt good about this, because at least it was clear that the district was taking data into account and doing their best to keep kids safe, even while dealing with lots of opposing views and pressure from some parents.

Amelia started the 2020–2021 school year with her virtual class, which had a few old friends and a few new friends. She loved her new teacher and was doing really well those first few weeks. The way it was structured for virtual learning at this point was that teachers took their classes through regular synchronous instruction in the mornings, and then in the afternoons, the students had asynchronous learning, where they were given a set of assignments or projects to complete.

It wasn't perfect, but Amelia was doing well with it. And every day, we heard about the fun activities her teacher put together. We felt fortunate to have Amelia in a class where the teacher was making such a great effort to bring kids together, even virtually.

By late September, the district informed us that changes were coming in October. Parents could decide at that point if they wanted to keep their students virtual or not, and those who chose in-person learning would be full-time in person, with appropriate masking and safety precautions.

It was a difficult decision for Erin and me to make, but given the overall risks at that point—and the fact that Amelia was doing OK with virtual schooling—we thought it was best to keep her virtual. We asked her opinion on the matter and Amelia also wanted to stay virtual, so it just felt like the right decision. This alone felt like a major win, since at this point in the pandemic, it felt like about 70 percent of a parent's job was the task of delivering crushing, disappointing news to our kids. (During normal times, maybe 45 percent, at best.)

A couple weeks later, Amelia suddenly came to me in my office, sat on my lap, and started crying. I was listening in on a virtual committee meeting online, but quickly yanked out my earbuds and asked what was wrong.

Through sobs, Amelia told me that her teacher told her that, with all the changes coming to the class structure the following week, this might be their last day together. With some kids returning to in-person classes and others staying remote, teachers and classes were being shuffled and changed.

My heart broke. Amelia loved her teacher. She had been thriving in her distance-learning environment, in no small part because of the work her teacher was doing. I would hear Amelia engage and participate, and she looked forward to school every day.

But now—on a dime—that was going to change. I held Amelia and cried with her. I remember the close bond I formed with so many of my teachers when I was in school, and I knew how sad this was for her. It is gut-wrenching as a parent to know and understand the pain your child is feeling but be completely powerless to do anything about it.

Amelia is strong, positive, and resilient. I knew that before the pandemic; going through it only underlined and boldfaced it. What

I remember feeling in that moment was *I know she is strong, I'm just tired of making her have to prove it all the time. I know she can handle this. I just wish she didn't have to.*

All decisions parents faced in those days were bad decisions. It was all about each family doing their best to choose the lesser evil. It was our choice as a family to keep Amelia in virtual learning for safety, but the result was losing her teacher. All we could do was decide the best way we knew how. But I felt real guilt and responsibility that our decision to keep her home created that hurt. Still, when cases had been raging, I also couldn't imagine sending her back.

Erin and I did our best to console our daughter. We told her that she was justified in feeling sad. We told her stories about times we had to change teachers. We also told her that she may love her new teacher just as much, but that doesn't mean she can't feel sad about having to deal with this change. Because she is awesome, she heard us, she absorbed it, and started to come around and cheer up a little.

One thing that helped was that Amelia had gotten a nice Target gift card from Grandma and Grandpa Schneider for her birthday, so Erin took her on a little shopping expedition to use it. When they returned, Amelia was thrilled to show off her haul: a couple of Barbie dolls, Play-Doh, LEGOs, and the game of Twister. Looking at all of it, I couldn't help but find it a little funny that literally everything she bought had also been popular when I was a kid, seemingly thousands of years ago. We were living through bizarre, mind-warping times, but some things do stay the same.

Erin had also brought back some candy, which is always the highlight of Henry's day. He had a few pieces and then asked me for another sucker.

"Buddy, I think that's enough sweets for one day," I said.

Henry groaned a low groan. He looked back at the box, then looked down and muttered, with incredible melodramatic emotion.

"Dad. You let me down. I want sucker."

Clearly, it was a day filled with parental letdowns, and Henry knew how to pile onto my guilt. I had to give him credit for pure maudlin drama on that one.

In the long run, Amelia did bounce back. She always does. She met her new teacher the following week, and before long was gushing about her. She went on to adore her new teacher and class, too. Some more of her old friends from first grade were in the virtual class with her, so there were lots of familiar faces.

Maybe there was something positive to be taken away from the fact that there are times when bad news can actually turn into good news. That's a lesson that is important for kids and grown-ups.

I'm not sure I'll ever fully understand the level of strength and resilience our kids showed during the pandemic. On some level, I know that I adapted to it but also was constantly processing the trauma, anxiety, and horror just to keep it together. I have little doubt I'll be walking that stuff off for years to come, as will much of humanity.

My hope is that it will make my children not fragile but, instead, much stronger. When I think about my own history and anxiety as a Gen Xer, my formative years were shadowed with the threat of nuclear war, so my generation is prone to fixate on big scary things that may not actually happen.

Like Twister, Barbies, and LEGOs, everything old is new again. We still probably face a vague threat of nuclear war, but I have to think the perspective of my kids' generation will be different because they lived in the shadow of things that definitely happened, not maybes.

And they survived it. And thrived. In my most positive moments, that is what I hold on to. Unlike me, who spent a lot of my life thinking any ill wind might knock me over, they might grow up understanding that no matter how dark the day, the sun still comes out on the next one.

DO YOU REMEMBER?

Injecting bleach to stop COVID? Adding to a list of fantastic "I'm-just-throwing-it out-there" ideas, that included nuking hurricanes and putting a shark-filled moat along the southern border of the United States, President Trump (in an April 2020 press conference) suggested that if UV light and topical disinfectants were good for killing the COVID virus on inert surfaces, why not in the human body?

Of course, most medical professionals would point out that the human body is substantially different than the average countertop and may have a negative reaction to harsh, poisonous chemicals being directly introduced into its inner workings.

This did inspire immediate statements from the manufacturers of many disinfectant products—whose communications departments were in disbelief of the necessity to write the words:

"Despite suggestions made by the President of the United States, please do not inject yourself with bleach."

Fortunately, very few people took this idea seriously, though there were a few cases of bleach injection that resulted in ER visits. Though to be fair, these might have been the kind of folks who would have tried this even without the president mentioning it.

CHAPTER 20

ELECTION DAZE

I once heard a quote that I, for years, have attributed to Mark Twain: "In Hell, every year is election year."

It's witty, it rings true, and sure sounds "Twain-y" (Mark, not Shania). Yet, when I went to look it up to get the wording right, I concluded that it's very likely Mark Twain never said any such thing.

So, I guess maybe *I* said it?

"In Hell, every year is election year." —Jim Schneider, author, Fencebat: A Big Kid's Guide to Parenting, Personal Growth, and Play

Hey, that looks pretty good. Apologies to Twain or whoever maybe said that first and put it out in the world for it to eventually seep into my brain.

Anyway, it would be our luck that the year the COVID pandemic was born, with all its associated stresses and challenges, it would also be an election year. The U.S. certainly has a long history of brutal and contentious elections; the trend line had been getting worse as the country became more divided—and 2020 was a doozy.

It was stressful in the lead-up, watching all the machinations, the screaming, the polls, the projections. No matter which candidate you supported, you were pretty convinced it would be the end of the world if the other one won the election. So, on top of the usual anger and arguments, there was also a weird pall of desperation surrounding the whole thing.

Our two ends of the political spectrum have long been living in separate worlds, but COVID *really* pushed us into separate universes, each complete with its own facts, news, and laws of physics.

Full disclosure, I am someone who voted for Joe Biden and lives in the world that elected Joe Biden. I am a Democrat, so those reading who think all Democrats are dangerous leftists who hate America, children, and apple pie, thanks for coming and I hope this tome will serve you well at your next book burning.

I frankly miss the days when you could have an actual conversation about policy and points of view, because I'm someone who believes that we need healthy debate and two strong political parties with different, productive ideas.

I actually had one of those conversations out of the blue at a conference in 2022 when I met a Montana Republican running for state office. It was jarring but also incredibly refreshing. No name-calling, no culture-war jingoism, just friendly and impassioned discussion and debate on policy. One of the things we talked about was the positive nature of government doing positive stuff, like facilitating infrastructure, fostering good education, and encouraging the growth of businesses. So much of politics today has turned into pro wrestling, with everyone yelling pointless platitudes into microphones to get social media attention. It was encouraging to talk to someone who might have different policy ideas but shared my passion for boring stuff like building a stable societal framework where everyone can benefit and grow.

Snoozer, right? Go figure. Both of us knew the other loved our country and wanted to do well by its people. Simple thing, but boy is it missing in our social fabric right now.

I voted for Joe Biden in the November 2020 election. Because I'm talking policy, I will skip over all the stuff about not liking Donald Trump and say, in all seriousness, that I voted on policy, as I always do. Foremost, I did not agree with the previous administration's handling of the COVID pandemic.

My issue was that even when the administration was trying to do some good things, the former president was constantly undercutting it by basically denying the pandemic existed. Again, the hellish coincidence of a pandemic occurring during an election year with a president who cared about literally *nothing* other than the election was not a great combination.

For example, the minute the former president chose to make wearing masks a political issue was a major turning point in the pandemic and in our culture. Instead of this being a moment where we all try to reasonably work together in the name of public health, it became just another choose-a-side game with people divided into camps of either taking COVID precautions seriously or saying masks are tyranny and stuff.

It really didn't have to be this way. We have gotten to a point where if one political party sees the other political party doing something, they assume it's bad. Look, where the pandemic is concerned, it's true that Liberals tended to think that masks and distancing were a good idea. So people who didn't like liberals instantly assumed that wasn't a good idea. But come on, not *everything* Liberals believe in is bad.

Are we wrong about some things? Absolutely. Like restaurants that specialize in small plates? Sure, not a great idea—you leave broke and still hungry. I get it. But masks and COVID precautions? Come on. There may have been something to that.

The election itself was, of course, a swirling mess of epic proportions. Leading up to it were the crazy debates, the whole thing with the president and first lady getting COVID, and Trump in the hospital, possibly having exposed his debate opponent when he refused to get tested.

It was all madness that future generations will struggle to comprehend. And the torture continued well past election day since it took nearly a week for all the results to be properly tabulated. At last, Joe Biden was declared the victor on November 7. I still remember it, because it happens to be my and Erin's anniversary. I was out for a run and saw texts coming in from my friends about the election being called.

I admit, I was relieved. Because I was at least hopeful for a change in tone and a more serious approach to the pandemic, foreign policy, and all the other policy preferences of mine. Over the next few months, I figured the "fake election" and "rigged" claims would fade out as the lawsuits and those filing them became more and more desperate and absurd. Even Republicans, most of whom hadn't yet developed the courage to publicly acknowledge Joe Biden as the president-elect, started making comments about how Trump just needed to get it out of his system.

I get it. Any parent knows the experience of having a child who gets upset by disappointment and needing time to kick, yell and moan to get through it. Typically, when they get a little older, our kids tend to grow out of those kinds of things. For others, it may take a little longer. Like 70 years longer.

But hey, no harm in some idle chatter, right? Sadly, that didn't turn out to be the case and we wound up with the whole January 6 horror show. Seeing the angry mob and rioters outside desecrating the halls of Congress — think *Star Trek* mirror universe meets *The Flintstones*—really struck me to the core. Erin and I watched it play out on TV in shock.

That moment was easily the most embarrassed I have ever been to be an American. And I am old enough to remember that time Roseanne Barr sang the national anthem and when the first President Bush threw up on the Japanese prime minister.

The aftermath of January 6 casts a long shadow on our country and society, in my humble opinion. A lot of us felt the disgust and shock of that moment. I really thought it would be enough to break the fever, but it wasn't. Within days, the divisions and separate realities took hold again, and each side left with their own story about January 6.

Recently, Amelia asked me some questions about the events of January 6, and I tried my best to explain. It wasn't easy, I admit. I try not to push my political beliefs on my kids because, ultimately, I want them to form their own opinions. I will say, however, that when explaining January 6, I felt fortunate to reside in the rational, down-to-earth world because it's hard to imagine explaining the other version.

In the world I live in: *Well, Amelia, there was this riot and attack on the Capitol. Why? Because the president lost the election but refused to believe it and didn't want to leave. So, he asked his supporters to come to Washington, D.C. He gave a speech, and a lot of the people there attacked the Capitol building and the people defending it in hopes of stopping Congress from certifying the election.*

In the other world: *Well, Amelia, President Trump really won the election by SO much, even though the other person got lots more votes. But all those votes were from China or Venezuela. So, Trump heroically told a huge, loving, and peaceful crowd to fight like hell! Not to literally fight, of course, but to "fight!" Peacefully. But fight! And then, some guys in the FBI and Antifa and Black Lives Matter started this terrible riot that was deadly and violent, but also super peaceful—not a big deal at all. The people who broke into the Capitol building were loving tourists, but also BLM instigators. It was horrible. But also, the people who stormed the Capitol were heroes and the ones arrested are political prisoners. Oh, and some people wanted to hang Mike Pence, which he probably deserved. I mean, have you seen that guy?*

I think the first way is way simpler. I'm lucky that our kids are young and only a little bit aware of politics and government right now. Because I often struggle to explain our current reality to *myself,* much less to young kids. I keep hoping maybe we'll find that way back to debates of substance that go deeper than calling the other person a traitor or whatever.

Sadly, if I could go back in time and talk to myself from five years ago, I would have probably believed that a common crisis, like COVID, would heal and unite our national divisions. I read *Watchmen* as a teenager and always assumed a big ugly worldwide threat would bring us together. Comic books lied to me. The opposite wound up being true, and now the fissures are even worse.

What will it take? I wish I knew the answer to that. Disease, war, and climate change haven't done it. Maybe we can all unite against small plates as a dining concept? It may not solve all problems, but a full and contented stomach is always a good first step.

DO YOU REMEMBER?

Presidential COVID? On October 2, 2020, the nation learned that the president and first lady both tested positive for COVID-19.

At the time, we were given many assurances that it was barely a sniffle for the president, who was airlifted to Walter Reed Medical Facility for care. There he staged numerous photo ops, doing things like signing a blank book and doing other things that, as anyone who has worked in an office knows well, were the affectations of someone trying to "look busy."

Both the president and first lady recovered, and rumor has it that President Trump had to be talked out of ripping his shirt open to reveal a Superman T-shirt underneath. This would have, of course, been in poor taste for many reasons. But also, it's safe to assume that no matter what a person's opinion of President Trump is, very few people want to see him take his shirt off.

CHAPTER 21

SEE THE BIRDS

One day, I took the kids to the park to enjoy a beautiful day, get outside, and have some fun. As we walked over, Henry started asking questions about what we were going to have for dinner that evening. As a point of context, it was about 10:30 in the morning.

I told him we were planning to have pasta, and he started getting upset because he didn't want pasta. I told him, "Look, it's not even close to dinner time, so let's not worry about it. We're about to go to the park and have fun, so let's focus on that."

We went a few rounds with this, and eventually he dropped the dinner thing—but not without a fight. I understand that, and always try to hear him. But I also don't want him to miss the good stuff because his focus is somewhere else. Erin and I also do our best to help coach him to enjoy the moment and not get hung up worrying about things that haven't even happened yet.

While on that walk, I was poring over the fact that Henry can sometimes get *so* caught up on something in the unwritten future. Then the hammer of realization pounded down on my thick skull.

Hold on, I sure do that, too.

I have suffered from some version of anxiety probably my whole life. Part of that is who I am, part of it is my brain's chemical makeup, and probably part of it was growing up a Gen Xer. But as I've worked on dealing with my anxiety in adult life, I've come to see its processes in my mind more clearly. And in the end, what is anxiety if not getting stuck on something in the unwritten future that hasn't even happened yet?

For me, anxiety is often inventing scenarios weeks, months, or years down the road and getting stuck on them in the present. I, too, often miss the moment because my mind is elsewhere. Is what I'm doing all that different than what Henry is doing when he worries about the prospect of a pasta dinner hours ahead?

I took that as a two-part lesson. For one, I should take a little of my own advice and try harder to be present and appreciate the moment instead of worrying about far-away potential problems. Secondly, this was a moment to recognize and understand how *real* these things are for Henry.

It can be difficult when he gets caught up on what cartoon he is going to watch or what snack he is going to have hours from now, but an important part of helping him through it is recognizing how big it feels to him, without minimizing it.

That was something to learn from and build from. I always want our kids to feel heard and understood. Even if it's just pasta. But let's be honest, the idea of looking upon a pasta dinner with anything other than excitement is outrageous. I also must work a little harder on teaching pasta appreciation, obviously.

Henry and I can both have trouble being in "the now" and being truly present, even if the things that pull us away are very different. One of the things I've worked to understand about my son is that we might process things differently sometimes, but there are also so many things I can relate to.

I look for opportunities where my kids and I can learn from each other. Henry has taught me many lessons about being present, as well. Some were pretty powerful. One such lesson took place when we were on that same stretch of sidewalk as the pasta-dinner-fixation episode. This time, I was walking Henry to Pre-K at the local school. In spring of 2021, we had eased him into a little bit of in-person Pre-K to get him some experience being in the classroom setting before he started kindergarten that fall. It was a drizzly, gloomy day but we decided to walk anyway. My mind was elsewhere, on some work problem or bills to pay or whatever the usual stuff is for me. I was distracted.

We grown-ups tend to have years and years of battle damage, fears, anxieties, and other head trash that clouds our vision. It's something I'm working on, but there are times when all the expert-recommended books, podcasts, and speakers you listen to are just the preamble to a lesson delivered simply by example and persistence; a lesson delivered by a five-year-old neurodiverse child.

On our walk, Henry was drawn to every puddle he saw because he loves, as he says, "jumping in muddy puddles." Other parents might recognize this as a popular *Peppa Pig* refrain, and indeed, that is a major contributor to Henry's puddle passion. But I also think he gets sensory stimulation out of the feeling, sound, and sensation of jumping in a puddle.

My mind of course always goes to *But your shoes will get dirty and wet!* He doesn't care. And for that day, I figured I wouldn't let myself care either. We had a nice walk and went for a little while in silence. Walking by the park near the school, Henry pointed and said, "Look at the birds!"

My mind was somewhere else, thinking about something insignificant. I gave the typical parental "Oh yeah, that's nice" kind of response. Thankfully, Henry was not having it. He was going to drag me into that moment.

"Dad, *see* the birds!" He said it with excitement I couldn't ignore.

There were four birds meandering around this large park space. I stopped with him for a second and watched the birds.

"I wonder if they're playing in the park," I said.

Henry liked the sound of that and said, "Yes, they like to play in the park."

We watched for another minute, and he asked if he could take a picture of the bird closest to us. I gave him my phone and helped him take a picture.

"It's a pretty bird," he said. It was.

We walked on, talking about the birds, and then Henry decided to track through the sand in the volleyball court. Once again, my first thought was about the cleanliness of his shoes. But he was in glee, feeling the sand as he tracked through it. Moments later, I realized I had gotten a couple steps ahead of him because he stopped to play with the petals that had fallen from the trees by the school. He soaked in that moment, too. And then was when I started to recognize my son was trying to teach me something.

I was focused on his shoes, on getting to school on time, and whatever else was clanging around in my head. I wasn't noticing the birds, the sand, the flowers, and just the beautiful stillness in the air. It was a gorgeous, rainy spring day, and I was missing it.

I dropped him off, and he was excited to run into his classroom. As I walked back, I thought a lot about this. I stopped for a moment and played with those flower petals. I tried to open up to what was around me. I wanted to experience what Henry experienced.

Earlier that morning, I had been listening to a podcast that was talking about the power of negative thoughts that pull us down. It wasn't advocating only thinking good thoughts all the time—that is, of course, impossible—but it called attention to the fact that on a subconscious level, many of us spend an extraordinary amount of effort on thoughts that aren't helpful or positive. It can both sap us of energy and cast a fog over the wonders right in front of us.

I definitely do that. I've made good progress toning down my internal critic, but a shocking amount of my daily internal monologue is still focused on what I might have messed up, will mess up, or can't get right. The speaker on the podcast was advocating for being more open to the positive and the world around us, which is so easily drowned out by that internal critic's ruckus.

That was on my mind as I continued the walk home. I scanned the park for the birds, and now there were none. I had a kind of metaphysical moment where I wondered *Was the power of my son's perception what brought the birds in the first place?* He first told me to look at the birds. And when I didn't, he told me to see them. *See* them. It took that command to get me there.

I tried for a moment to strip away all of the noise and just be in that moment. I felt something lift inside of me. I had been working hard, through writing, mindfulness, and meditation, to try to connect with some kind of universal energy greater than myself—and for a moment, I could actually feel it. The best way I could describe it was it was like I was rising like a balloon, feeling tethered to everything around me. For what I'm sure was just a few seconds, I was overwhelmed to the verge of tears.

For those seconds, I was on the doorstep of real connection, when I could suddenly feel the *You can't* and *You won't* voices whisper inside—and I very distinctly felt the balloon being pulled down. I was able to resist the negative voices, almost with a laugh, *Guys! Not now!* But their mere presence had already popped that balloon, descending me back down to Earth.

I walked on, still feeling good and appreciative of the moment, but the fleeting glimpse of something greater had passed on. And that was the moment I realized I had actually grown. I didn't feel disappointment in the fact that I got so close to an epiphany and got yanked down, but hopeful to know that there is something there. I understand now why masters meditate for years in search of moments like that. I was fortunate to have Henry to guide me into a moment at a most unexpected time.

And the birds. Maybe it's just that I read a lot of Carlos Castañeda in college, so I believe that birds always show up with purpose. And plenty of spiritual thought around the world agrees.

I wrote about this in my blog. My usual process was to always write posts one day removed, reflecting on the previous day. Seeing the birds was a rare instance where I got home and wrote it down immediately, because I didn't want to forget. But even then, I could already feel the experience fading away a little. It stuck with me a while, but this is another story I probably would have forgotten, lost in the memory hole, had I not written it down.

I guess if I could pass on anything from those two experiences, it's the importance of being present. That day at the park, I helped Henry release the worry of future pasta, and he wound up getting back to the moment and having a great time at the park. On that walk, Henry taught me not just to look, but to see. I saw the birds, I saw the rain, I saw it all—and it was wonderful. Fleeting though it was, I was in that moment. And it was perfect.

EXCERPT FROM JIM'S ABANDONED BOOK OF COVID KNOCK-KNOCK JOKES

Knock knock!
Who's there?
Flattening the curve.
Flattening the curve who?
Doesn't matter, that never happened anyway.

CHAPTER 22

RAISIN HELL

In May of 2021, Erin was in the process of launching her brand-new business, Mountain Summit Coaching, to help families of children with disabilities find their way forward. It was an exciting time and she poured herself into networking and into building the basic infrastructure of her new venture.

She lined up a photoshoot with a local photographer to take photos for her new website. We had lots of work to do around the house before the photographer arrived. Erin and I went to a local nursery to get some plants for our garden planter and backyard flowerpots. We figured, if we were having any outdoor shots taken, it would be better if things didn't look dead and desolate—we weren't aiming for an *Addams Family* aesthetic. Definitely something less mysterious and spooky, and altogether ooky.

Erin handled the planting, and I cleaned up the house to get things shipshape and presentable. Everything was going pretty smoothly, and Erin went up to get ready while I finished some last-minute tidying up before go time.

This photoshoot served dual purposes: get some professional images for Erin's website and, while the photographer was here, take some family photos.

Everyone has experienced the stress and insanity of family portraits, whether it was as a kid watching your parents freak out about having everything just so or as a parent, wrangling and micromanaging everything just to get your kids to have a somewhat-normal smile and wear a decent shirt for five minutes.

We had that going on, with the additional layer of really wanting to capture some good images for Erin's professional material. Also, this was still a time when having someone we didn't know come into the house felt a little stressful and scary. Suffice to say, I was feeling a smidge on edge as we got ready.

We'd had this on the calendar for weeks and the nervousness was not new, but we were hoping it would go well. The two big X factors that day were (1) the weather and (2) Henry. Both were difficult to predict with any real accuracy. We were hoping for a day sunny enough to take some pictures outside, but not so sunny that everything would be washed out. And we also hoped Henry would be in a good enough mood to cooperate and be game for some family photos.

This can be the case with many kids, and certainly with Henry, but when he digs his heels in and decides he doesn't want to do something, you might as well try to ask the Grand Canyon not to be a canyon. *Hey, I need to get to the other side, can you just close it up? Thanks. Appreciate it.*

Well, about an hour before the shoot, the weather was looking like it could storm any minute. *OK, deep breath. We'll adjust. Maybe it'll blow over.* Then the kids came home from spending a few hours at their grandparents' house. And as soon as he got out of the car, Henry was angry and pouting about the fact that he got to me about four seconds after Amelia did, because *HE* wanted to be the one to tell me they had a fun day.

OK, things weren't looking great on the Henry front. He seemed kind of tired and cranky. *But all right, we can roll with this,* I thought. Staying calm, I figured I had an hour to get him soothed and settled down to a point where he could hopefully take at least a few pictures. I got him a snack, and he immediately asked to watch the California Raisins in *Will Vinton's Claymation Christmas Celebration.*

For those of you who don't remember, and I imagine that is most of you, the Claymation® production company produced an obscure Christmas special back in the late 1980s, starring the then fabulously popular California Raisins. My siblings and I had watched it as kids, and I always had a soft spot for it. I had showed the Christmas special to my kids the previous holiday season, to rave reviews.

Henry loved it, and he tends to watch things he loves repeatedly. Also, he is very much OK with watching holiday specials year-round. *It's the Great Pumpkin, Charlie Brown* has been on a continuous loop at our house for about four years.

But, whatever. *Sure thing, buddy. Let's do it. Watch anything you like.* I fired up the raisins for him. At this point, it's important to note that this particular holiday special isn't available on any streaming or digital service—it is only available on VHS or DVD. And we had a rare DVD copy. File this information away for later.

I hit play on the old DVD player. Nothing. No light, no whirring whine of the disc spinning—just silence. As luck would have it, this day of all days was the day that our DVD player, which we've had for years, decided to die.

It wouldn't power on. It was just dead. I broke the news to Henry and asked if we could watch something else. He immediately started to cry . . . A LOT. Like, he really broke down. This was exploding quickly and badly. Erin and I were scrambling, trying to see if there was anything else he could watch, but no. It had to be the California Raisins.

I suddenly remembered we had a *very* old DVD/VCR combo unit collecting dust in the basement. I ran down to see if I could make that work. The first thing I noticed is this model was way before HDMI cables, so I also had to dig around to find some old RCA cables to use to even connect it to any TV.

Shockingly, I was able to locate some and managed to get the old player up and running. Success! We were in the homestretch now. I excitedly told Henry when it hit me: I still had to get the disc out of the old player, which was now just a powerless hunk of metal and plastic, imprisoning the California Raisins DVD in its iron grasp.

I tried to pull out the DVD tray, and that would not budge. So, there we were—like, twenty minutes before the photoshoot we were preparing for all day—Henry in full-screaming meltdown, and I was struggling to pry apart an old DVD player with a screwdriver and my bare hands, in hopes of extracting a fragile, precious-to-my-son, difficult-to-replace copy of an 80s Christmas special in the vague hope of soothing my son, who was still bawling his eyes out.

Yup. Just like we planned it.

I did get it *partially* taken apart. Then, I spent the next several minutes trying to carefully pry open the tray so I could somehow slide out the disc without breaking it. It was clamped in there. I needed to use sufficient force to get it out, but not too much that it would break the disc in half.

This surgery was both delicate and brutal.

But eventually I managed to get it out. Huzzah! I put the disc in the ancient DVD/VCR, and then discovered the remote control didn't work. Of course. I figured it was the batteries, so I opened the panel to find the batteries had corroded and melted, completely destroying the remote control in a pool of acid.

Sigh.

I had to use the rudimentary controls on the physical console to manually fast-forward through an even less well-known Halloween special on the disc to get to the Christmas one Henry wanted to watch. As the opening strains of "Deck the Halls" came through the speaker, Henry was at relative peace at last.

Just then, the photographer arrived, and we frantically finished getting ready.

In spite of this insane preamble, the photoshoot went remarkably well. After all that drama, Henry wound up being amazing. He cooperated, joked around with the photographer, had fun, and was his happy, goofy self. Amelia was also great. And the photographer did a wonderful job working with both of them. We got some amazing pictures that are still some of my favorite family photos.

Part of the adventure of parenting is not knowing what piece of electronic equipment you might need to rip apart and what obscure decades-old holiday special you might need to watch to soothe one of your kids. Every day is a bagful of surprises.

The kinds of high-stress, chaotic moments, like the one I had with Henry and the California Raisins DVD, are a part of life. Anyone who has kids, has tried to host an event, has had a wedding, or has in any way been involved in an "important" day where you just want everything to be perfect knows that things never quite go that way.

It's hard to handle those crazy turns, but it's also important to hold on to the fact that all crazy moments pass, and nothing is truly "ruined." It's all part of what makes life memorable. It's not easy, but I've certainly learned if you can teach yourself to be OK with a little chaos here and there, you'll be a lot more at peace when the winds blow.

A PICTURE IS WORTH 1,000 WORDS

One of the photographs taken following the episode with the California Raisins DVD appears in this book. The family photo on the Dedication page was taken less than an hour after the events described in this chapter. As difficult as parts of that day were, the result was a picture that captures the love and joy that binds our family together. It clearly demonstrates that the space between chaos and beauty is very thin. All people and all families struggle, but hard moments are never the end. There are smiles and laughter to be found on the other side.

CHAPTER 23

MAGIC KINGDOM

There were so many times that I thought that COVID was "over," or at very least, on its last legs. But like Frankenstein's monster, every time you thought it was down, it would come grunting back.

Burn it in a windmill, blow it up in a castle, knock it into a pit of burning sulfur, it doesn't matter. It just comes back angrier and often played by a less prominent actor.

The first time I thought we were on the glide path out was in the summer of 2021. Vaccines were available to adults, and while we were still waiting on the kids' version, we at least felt a slight easing of cases. Feeling that, perhaps, life might be pseudo-normal sooner rather than later.

That June, I even took the step of ending my daily "Parenting, Productivity, and Quarantine" blog after 450 consecutive posts. I thought it was a nice round number, and after all, the COVID story was over, right?

Am I right?

No, I wasn't right.

Back it came. In the fall, the roller coaster of cases went up and down once again. Like the rest of the world, we were exhausted of it all. Still, we continue taking precautions, wearing masks, and doing the things we needed to do to keep the kids safe.

Late in the year was the loudest and lamest Frankenstein sequel yet.

Finally, the vaccine for kids five and older was available. We scrambled right away to get our kids appointments as soon as humanly possible. Even amidst some skepticism among some out there, "Gee, are you sure the vaccines are—"

"YES. They are safe. They are good, let's go. No need to finish that sentence."

We scheduled vaccinations for the kids just as soon as the appointments opened up. Erin scoured the Denver metro area for the first available appointments and found one at a Children's Hospital branch on the opposite side of town. No problem. We took a trek down there.

It was a particularly windy fall afternoon, and the vaccinations were conducted in a big coach bus in the parking lot. It was good the hospital was being very careful about distancing and safety, but also bad because we had to explain to two kids, who were already hesitant about getting shots, that we had to stand around enduring gale-force winds in a parking lot and wait for those shots.

Before long, we were on the bus. Erin and I each took a kid in our laps to get the shot. Being on this tricked-out bus where people were walking around with masks and needles, I felt like I was touring with the Rolling Stones in the early '70s.

I was worried about how the kids were going to do with the shot, as their general history with them had not been good. No matter where on earth you are, if you're walking around and hear a distant, shrill shriek echoing, it's possible it's the sound of one of my children getting a shot.

But for whatever reason, this one went really smoothly. I had Henry on my lap, and the nurse did a great job talking and distracting him while getting ready to administer the vaccine. When the nurse administered the shot, he did it with such lightning speed that Henry's only reaction was, "Hey! What are you doing?" No scream, no cry. Just something that sounded like a line from Arnold on *Diff'rent Strokes*.

With at least one vaccine dose in for the kids, we felt like we could finally start talking about something we had long wanted to do as a family: taking a trip to Disneyland. COVID had cooped us up and canceled numerous trips, vacations, and other activities. However, with a fully vaccinated family on the near horizon, Erin and I thought it was time to let loose and have a little fun.

Looking at the timing of the kids' vaccinations, we estimated they would be fully vaccinated on Christmas Day. Perfect. We booked flights, bought tickets, and made our plans for a big holiday surprise for the kids—a trip to California the week between Christmas and New Year's. It was all running like clockwork. What could go wrong?

Omicron.

We made these plans in November. By early December, we started hearing rumblings of this scary, new strain of COVID that was spreading like wildfire. It's funny, looking back, I think I was having some of the same déjà vu from the initial Omicron spike as I had to the original arrival of COVID-19 almost two years prior. It was worrying, but I somehow felt like *Ah, it won't be all THAT bad, right?*

The closer we got to Christmas, the more it felt like the only entity that might travel the world quicker and visit more homes than Santa Claus that holiday season might be the Omicron variant. We were holding our breath that we might make it into the new year uninfected so we could take this trip.

The narrative was that everyone has it, is getting it, and it might be a little crazy to travel. We had to grapple with diametrically opposing instincts. Again, we were never big risk-takers with COVID, but it became difficult to determine what acceptable risk was here. *Should we cancel the trip like we did with all those trips in 2020? Should we chance it and move forward? Would that be that reckless?*

This weighed on me all the way up 'til Christmas. We had our graphic designer friend make us these great Disneyland tickets to wrap up and give to the kids. I would see those hidden in my office cabinet, taunting me. Like Mr. Sulu said from *Star Trek II: The Wrath of Khan*, "Not going to make it, are we?"

In the days leading up to Christmas, pretty much my entire family back in Wisconsin wound up with Omicron. My anxious self was starting to feel that it was more like *when* than *if* we would get it.

My mind started racing, wondering which scenario would be worse: getting COVID just before we were due to leave and having to cancel the trip, or actually getting COVID *in* California and being confined to a random Marriott in Anaheim, with Disneyland just out of reach.

If Dante didn't include that as a Circle of Hell, he should have.

As of Christmas Day, our merry band seemed just fine, and the kids were super excited about our upcoming trip to Disneyland. As we had at other times in the pandemic, Erin and I ultimately made the calculation that this virus could be with us a while, so we need to try to do what we can to venture out, safely as possible.

We ordered a bunch of KN95 masks, which were a hip, new, and hard-to-find thing at the time. Everything we knew about Omicron said the old-school cloth masks weren't going to cut it anymore, so we decided to step it up.

A day or two before we left, I felt a dry throat and started freaking out. *Dammit! What if I'm the weak link that ruins this whole trip?*

I took a home test and fortunately tested negative. Then later, I read something about how being anxious can dry out your throat. Go figure.

In the end, we made it to California. The kids are great travelers and did well on the flight, masks and all. We spent the first couple of days staying with a friend in Los Angeles, and our first theme park visit was to Universal Studios.

With Omicron running rampant, the park required masks, which we were relieved about. We went mostly to see the Wizarding World of Harry Potter, which was super cool. What wasn't as cool was that we happened to be there on a rare, very rainy day in Los Angeles.

There were some high points, like Amelia being picked by the Wand Master in Ollivanders Wand Shop and taking part in a fun wand selection exercise. Henry really enjoyed the *Secret Life of Pets* ride. We bought plastic ponchos and tried our best to enjoy the day. It was mighty cold and soggy, but we had fun.

Looking back, that day at Universal Studios strikes me as the perfect encapsulation of the whole strange COVID era. One of the few family photos we have from that day shows the four of us by Hogwarts, bundled up in clear plastic ponchos and KN95 masks. We look like we were visiting the Chernobyl Exclusion Zone, not Universal Studios. If I could go back in time and share this photo with my childhood self, he would undoubtedly reply "Hmm, so that nuclear war we were all worried about *did* come after all."

Fortunately, we had much better weather for our three-day visit to Disneyland later that week. Being there on New Year's Eve, New Year's Day, and the day after wound up being perfect. We got to usher in 2022 with amazing fireworks and music. After being isolated for so long, it felt both surreal and wonderful to take part in a real communal event like that again.

Plus, in retrospect, we got to visit Disneyland during a sweet spot that was just a few months after several lockdowns had ended and just before the time when a bunch of weirdo protesters started hanging around outside all Disney parks, shouting about grooming and stuff. Sometimes it's better to be lucky than good, as the saying goes.

We still wore masks indoors and outdoors, even though it was not required outdoors there. I would say the majority of folks at Disneyland wore masks at all times. With the benefit of hindsight, I'm not convinced it was necessary for us to wear masks outside, but so little was known about Omicron at the time, people were being extra cautious. It really seemed that, like Beetlejuice, you could conjure Omicron just by uttering its name. We didn't want to chance it near big crowds.

It was a gamble for our family, in more ways than one. First of all, deciding to go was absolutely a risk in the face of this Omicron surge. Secondly, we had no idea how Henry would react to this kind of overwhelming experience. These were both big chances that could have opted us to just stay home. But in the end, our philosophy tends to be to try to take measured risks.

As far as Omicron was concerned, we made it through the whole trip with no issue. We did play it very, very safe. We wore masks everywhere. We went into one restaurant where we noticed the staff wasn't wearing masks, so we took our food to-go and ate at our hotel. It might have been fine, but as I mentioned before, the last thing we wanted was to get sick while we were there.

And for Henry, he did great. Was it perfect? Heck no. But we got through it quite well. We spent a lot of time preparing him and talking through things with him. On the first day, he hit a few bumps, but did amazingly well. On our second day, he was tired and overwhelmed, so we took turns letting him play in areas where he felt more comfortable and helped coach him through the experience.

Even looking at that postapocalyptic photo of us at Universal makes me smile. Even with the lead-up stress and the exhaustion of walking around those days, it was a wonderful trip—one that never would have happened if I had appeased my inner paranoia and hermit behavior.

Henry's favorite rides were Splash Mountain and Pirates of the Caribbean. Amelia loved the Cars ride in California Adventure, and gave rave reviews to many other rides, including Dumbo, Gadget's Go-Coaster and the Ferris wheel on Pixar Pier.

She was decidedly not so much a fan of Splash Mountain. I don't claim to know how the physics of these rides work. We all got wet, sure, but somehow about 75 percent of the water that hit our entire family seemed to wind up in Amelia's lap. She left the ride soaked to the bone and cold. It put us in a pickle, but here's a pro tip to those traveling to Disneyland. You may not know this, but it turns out that if you need a new shirt or any number of other clothing items, they actually have stores at the park that sell those things. Quite a few, really. They really are everywhere.

Obviously, Disney knows what it's doing, because along with the rides, the kids had a wonderful time loading up on every piece of merchandising imaginable. Such that we needed to buy an entirely separate suitcase just to get that stuff home. Though my favorite Henry moment from the trip was walking one evening with him around the California Adventure park. It was getting a little chilly, and as we were walking by a gift shop, I asked, "Henry, would you like to buy a sweatshirt?"

He shrugged and said, "No Dad. I have a sweatshirt at home."

That's my boy.

Our entire visit to Disneyland was indeed magical. It was a great bonding experience as a family, and we were all able to go out and be silly kids together. We laughed and joked, we reviewed each ride and attraction and created memories we still reference together almost daily. It was a scary time to travel, but I'm happy to say that in the risk/reward breakdown, this trip wound up being high on the reward side.

We were not reckless. We took every reasonable precaution we could. But we also decided to tolerate a risk and swing for the fences a little. I'm very glad we did, because it gave us amazing memories and an adventure we could all share together.

Those moments when I'm afraid to step out, I think of *The Lord of the Rings*.

It's a dangerous business, Frodo, going out your door. You step onto the Road, and if you don't keep your feet, there's no knowing where you might be swept off to.

We took those steps, kept our feet, and were swept off to someplace good. We also knew better than to pick up random rings in caves.

DO YOU REMEMBER?

Vaccine microchips? While many excitedly awaited the approval and distribution of a COVID-19 vaccine to help save lives, protecting the population from the continued spread of the virus, some saw it as yet another plot in a tangled web of conspiracies.

Many believed wild claims that the vaccine would implant you with microchips that would allow Bill Gates to—for some reason—track and control you. It has, of course, been common knowledge for many years that Bill Gates has keen interest in tracking the movements of small-town folks in rural America . . . I guess so he can know which Casey's gas station they'll hang out at on a Friday night.

Others claimed the vaccines would make people magnetic, which possibly upped the appeal of the vaccine for comic book nerds who always dreamed of being Magneto from X-Men.

Of course, these battles and conspiracies continued months and years after the vaccine's release, giving Americans yet another thing to argue and scream at each other about.

CHAPTER 24

UNCONVENTIONAL SWING

"What the heck is that?"

Through a ring of trees, I saw streaks of the kind of bright, primary colors that one often sees on playgrounds. The colors of whimsy and ultra-durable plastic.

Our walk had been quiet, strolling down an unfamiliar path in a familiar place. But now we heard the distinct sounds of kids' laughter and detected a kind of lateral movement at least eight feet off the ground. It felt like a *Jurassic Park* moment, with something big and undefined moving at unnatural speed just out of sight.

We all stopped and stared. The nearby hoots and laughter continued.

"Let's go THERE," Amelia said.

•   •   •

Backing up.

It was the spring of 2021, and we were approaching the first real *Hey, COVID is going away . . . PSYCHE!* period of the pandemic. There would, of course, be several of those.

We were in Avon, a small mountain town about fifteen minutes up Highway 70 from Vail. A little more low-key than its well-known neighbor, Avon feels notably relaxed, and at least there we weren't the only ones who wear off-the-rack clothes and drive a sub-luxury automobile.

By this point, Erin and I had both had our first vaccine doses but were still taking it super cautious. We hadn't traveled very much during the pandemic and were trying to find ways to get out into the world carefully.

We'd been to Avon plenty in the Before Times. We had our routine of places we liked to eat, things we liked to do, and places we would visit, etc. A lot of our usual haunts still felt pretty iffy, either because of actual closures or because we didn't feel comfortable being in big crowds.

A couple weeks before our trip to Avon, we had taken the really gutsy step of going to the outdoor pool in our neighborhood. The pool had been closed for all of 2020 and had just opened up for the first time since. Hesitant at first, this was another of those baby steps forward in a time of caution.

While there, we saw other actual human beings from our neighborhood. These were folks we used to see all the time, out and about or at school pick-ups, but hadn't encountered in months. Everyone had the excited, yet faraway look in their eyes. The look indicative of people who had been through a lot, were thrilled to have some human contact, but weren't entirely sure how it worked anymore.

We were talking about summer plans with one of our neighbors and mentioned our upcoming trip to Avon, and how we used to go there all the time. She asked if we'd ever been to the lake.

What lake?

It's funny that you can visit a place so many times and not realize what's right under your nose. After that conversation, we looked it up on a map and, sure enough, Lake Nottingham was about a five-minute walk from the hotel where we normally stay. Somehow, with the way the streets and topography of the area are laid out, we had never noticed it was even there.

Jumping back to our visit to Avon, with lots of our usual haunts and routine still not feeling great, we took the opportunity to explore. One morning, we excitedly told the kids we were going for . . . wait for it . . . A WALK!

"Can we go to the toy store?" Amelia asked.

"No, we're taking a walk around a really pretty lake."

"How pretty?"

"Will it take loooong?" Henry moaned.

If our lives were an '80s sitcom, "Will it take loooong?" would be Henry's catchphrase. And it would appear on buttons, stickers, ringer T-shirts, and be the basis of a terrible novelty rap song.

After many attempts at convincing the kids that this was a fun activity, Erin and I finally just said, "We're going." I had really tried to sell them on the idea. I had worked in sales for four years—never loved it. All techniques I learned failed miserably anyway with two small kids, whose favorite parts about going to the mountains were the toy store and ice cream.

Features and benefits sure don't work. And with a kid like Henry, the good old reverse psychology trick sure doesn't work:

Well, this walk probably isn't for you after all.

That's right! he'd say. Henry'd call the bluff.

Still, the grown-ups are ultimately in charge and after a little bit of whining, we were off to the lake. And I will say, the fresh mountain air tends to purify even Amelia and Henry. Before long, they settled in and were enjoying the new scenery.

We found Nottingham Lake, and it was beautiful. Just a small, gentle mountain lake, ringed by trees and ridges. Bits of snow still dotted the peaks, and the still water glistened a vibrant blue that you see at these kinds of elevations. It's like the water knows how close to the sky it is.

The kids ran around a big open field, chasing each other, laughing, and being free of all the confinement and anxiety of the previous months. We all felt a sense of relief, and even I was able to shed my anxiety for a little while.

It was on our walk back to the hotel that we spied strange movements in the trees.

"Let's go THERE," Amelia said.

So we did. When we got closer, we saw what all the fuss was about. It was indeed a big playground, complete with climbing towers, big, covered slides, and a crazy swing that was the source of much of the excitement.

This was a truly outside-the-box, mad-scientist, brilliant, and unconventional swing.

There was a small platform with ramps on either side, and a large metal support ring—probably about thirty feet in diameter—made a circular path from one side back to the other. The ring was a track for this suspended swing, which ran on it like some kind of upside-down monorail.

A kid would get on the platform and into the swing, push down, and the swing would glide along the path, in an up and down weaving motion, while the kid in the swing pulled the chains and pumped their legs in a traditional swing motion, that just happened to work with the forward motion of the track. The rider's legs dangle, and they fly.

It was wild. The kids were mesmerized. This kid was, too.

The playground was not crowded, but we were still a little hesitant to get too close to people. A couple families with their kids, a few older and a few younger, were taking their turns on the swing.

I know what you're thinking, *You were outside! It was safe, come on.* It's true. Knowing more today, I would agree with that. Even then, I was getting more comfortable with that idea. But after a year of caution with two unvaccinated and unprotected kids, I still wasn't sure how to relinquish my hold. But this was a moment where my grip eased a little bit.

While I was fascinated by the swing, and having doubts about approaching other people, my kids were both drawn to and scared of this whimsical contraption. After a minute or two, Erin cut through all the hesitation with a gentle, encouraging smile and said, "Come on. Let's do it."

We walked up and Amelia found the courage to be the first. She got on that swing, hanging on so tightly I thought the chains might break.

"Ready, Amelia?" I asked.

"Ready, Daddy!" she replied. And I pushed her off the platform.

Wooosh! She was off and screaming with delight. It was a rush, and we all laughed, feeling a release of all the isolation and fear from the last year.

Henry soon had his turn, and we were all laughing and having fun with the other kids and families there, each patiently waiting their next turn on the swing.

And the swing, by the way, would run out of momentum just before the platform, so it would be up to me and the other grown-ups to grab it and pull it back to the ramp. I found myself darting around the whole thing, pulling up the swing for my kids and others. I was so full of energy and joy in that moment, I was just zipping around before realizing how winded I felt.

Eventually, the other families went on their way, and it was just us for a little while. At that point, I felt like it was my turn. I got on the swing and let the kids push me off.

I can still feel the smile I had, and I shouted out just like Amelia did on her first turn. It was a rush of sincere, pure joy and fun.

Our usual routine in Avon changed as a result of the pandemic. When we traveled there, or anywhere, things were not the same. We were forced to find new paths, and had we not followed one, I don't know if we ever would have found that beautiful mountain lake or the delightfully unconventional swing.

Now that swing is part of our routine when we go to Avon. We even started staying in a place that's closer to that park, and it's one of the things we most look forward to on our visits.

COVID reset the world we live in. I spent a lot of time at the beginning wondering *When can we go back to the Before Times?* But the truth is, those days are gone now. It doesn't mean there isn't joy to be found in new places in our new world. Sometimes it just takes exploring a new path, taking something as ancient and tried-and-true as a swing, and doing it just a little bit differently.

ACKNOWLEDGMENTS

There are many people who helped me bring this book to life.

First and foremost, I want to thank my incredible wife, Erin, for her endless support and encouragement in what was a challenging project in challenging times. Her insight and wisdom not only helped steer our entire family through the pandemic but also inspired me to grow as an individual along the way. She encouraged my writing the P's & Q blog and for years has told me that I should be writing books. At long last, I have. Thank you, Erin, for having faith in me even when I haven't, and for being my inspiration and my partner in this and all journeys.

I also must express infinite gratitude to the real stars of this story, my superhero teammates, spaceship crewmates and adventure partners, Amelia and Henry. Reflecting on everything I've done in my life, nothing ranks anywhere near the honor of being the father of these two amazing individuals. Amelia's boundless positivity, empathy, and love, as well as Henry's courage, humor, and sense of wonder are sources of endless light in my life. Thank you both for always showing me new things, for letting me play make-believe with you and for keeping me as young as a fellow of my age can be.

Reflecting on our family's journey during the time chronicled here, I must also give a sincere thank you to Henry's therapy support team. Not only did you work wonders with him during the most challenging of times, you became part of our family and helped to guide us to better understand our son and each other. To Maddie,

Kayla, Michael, Amanda and Victor and everyone else who helped along the way, we are eternally grateful.

Thanks to the writers in my life for being sounding boards for me and inspiring me with your own incredible work. To Dave and Tom, two writers I've worked with and respected mightily for 30 years, who have always encouraged and challenged me to grow and improve in my craft. To Erika, a fellow traveler and longtime friend who has always supported and encouraged me to find my creative voice. To Kallin and Heather, my fellow "Write Club" members, for reminding me of the importance of workshopping and being part of a community of writers. To Tom and Katie for contributing to my blog during the depths of COVID; I hope you'll both tell your stories someday, too. And to Christina, John, Gilbert, Wanda, Amanda, Laurie, Jason, Shelley, Wendy, and all the others I've written for and with professionally over the years, and who have given me the confidence to call myself "a writer."

Gratitude and thanks to my fantastic team at Rogue Publishing, without whom I'd never have gotten to this point. First off, thanks to Kerrie who pointed me in the direction toward self-publishing this work. To Susie, my sherpa on this quest, thank you for all your insight and for lighting the way for me. Thanks to Carla for your excellent design, Lisa and Lindsay for your help in editorial, and Natalie for your keen photographic eye. Gratitude also to longtime friend and web designer extraordinaire, Kristin, for all your help with logos, websites, etc. I never could have made the original P's & Q blog run without your help.

Also, a very special thank you to my editor, Nadia, for your feedback, suggestions, and all you did to help me shape this book. I knew I needed help crafting the raw material I had into a more complete work. As a one-time editor myself, I hoped to connect with someone who would understand what I was trying to say and help me communicate it in an effective way. I couldn't have asked for a better partner in that endeavor, and I thank you so much for your honesty and insight.

Apologies if I missed anyone here, and if I did, I'll be sure to give you an extra shout out in the sequel to this book: *Fencebat II: The Empire Strikes Bat*.

Finally, thanks to everyone who read my P's & Q blog in 2020 and 2021, and all the friends, family, and colleagues who have encouraged me as a writer over the years and decades. Whether kind words or constructive criticism, it all was important in my growth as a person and as a scribe.

To this day, one of my proudest moments as a writer was during the production of a student film I co-wrote with my friend Eddie in graduate school back in the 1990s. Legendary comedian Shelley Berman was on set and in the scene, as he delivered what was one of my favorite gags in the screenplay, he stopped and said, "What kind of hack writes this crap?"

This kind of hack. Thank you for the feedback, Shelley. That taught me that a good writer knows when to accept a piece of criticism and when to stand up for your work. With all due respect to Mr. Berman's storied career, I defend that line to this day.

It stayed.

ABOUT THE AUTHOR

A writer, husband, and father to two young children, Jim Schneider began his career at age 17 as a disc jockey on an AM polka radio station in Wisconsin. He has gone on to work as an editor and writer for numerous national magazines in a variety of subject areas, including sustainability, architecture, construction, education, and sports. Jim is the executive director of a regional construction trade association in Colorado, has a passion for sustainable design and construction, and educates architects and engineers in the mountain states.

When COVID-19 came on the scene and the world shut down, Jim started a blog called *P's & Q: Parenting, Productivity & Quarantine*. From March of 2020 through June of 2021, he posted each day his experiences and perspectives on being a working parent navigating difficult times for his kids, his family, his job, and the world in general.

During the pandemic, Jim's son Henry was identified as being autistic, inspiring his whole family to educate themselves about neurodiversity and the challenges often faced by individuals with disabilities. Jim now writes about disability parenting topics for publications like *Colorado Parent* magazine.

Jim lives in Denver with his wife, Erin, and children Amelia and Henry. He continues to write about sustainability, construction, parenting, and disability support and is developing a new content initiative called "Parenting in Hell," dedicated to helping parents raise positive kids in a negative world. Look for Parenting in Hell in early 2023.

To learn more about Jim and his work, visit writer-schneider.com.

www.ingramcontent.com/pod-product-compliance
Lightning Source LLC
Chambersburg PA
CBHW030252130626
46549CB00002B/492